MEN
AND
WOMEN
OF
CHRIST

Neal A. Maxwell

BOOKCRAFT
Salt Lake City, Utah

Library of Congress Catalog Card Number: 91–70121

ISBN 0–88494–785–8

4th Printing, 1993

Printed in the United States of America

Contents

Acknowledgments

Special appreciation is extended to friends Liz Haglund and Roy Doxey, who once again were willing to review an early draft during the summer and to make suggestions. Luke Ong was most helpful with computer readouts having to do with the "Questions of the Lord." Excellent editing then followed by George Bickerstaff, who blended precision and patience in his suggestions.

Cory Maxwell encouraged this effort as he offered candor and love. As ever, Susan Jackson patiently endured several drafts, always being accommodating.

This is not an official Church publication. Hence, even though I was helped in its preparation, I alone am responsible for the views it expresses.

—

CHAPTER 1

"Begin to Be Enlightened"

As we look about us we perceive that unfortunately some Church members are in the "broad" way; most are scattered all along the straight and narrow path. The enlightened are moving forward steadily toward becoming men and women of Christ (see 3 Nephi 27:27; Helaman 3:29–30). Others are moving, but only irregularly. Some are dawdling. Still others are milling round the exits and entrances. A few have turned back or been turned aside.

Rather than describe members "geographically," however, let us view their variety "attitudinally."

Some members, undecided about taking on serious discipleship, continue with the "multitudes in the valley of decision" (Joel 3:14). It is ironical that this wearing indecisiveness produces its own form of fatigue. Moreover, those who fret and stew over whether or not to be "enlisted till the conflict is o'er" (*Hymns*, no. 250) are already losing the battle.

If we enlist and take the Savior's yoke upon us we "shall find rest unto [our] souls" (Matthew 11:29). If we are only part-time soldiers, though, partially yoked, we experience quite the opposite: frustration, irritation, and the absence of His full grace and spiritual rest. In that case weaknesses persist and satisfactions are intermittent. The less involved members resemble cartoonist Bill Mauldin's proud garritroopers of World War II—those who were too far forward to wear ties, but too far back to get shot, yet regarded themselves as real soldiers in the midst of the fray! Actually the partially yoked experience little spiritual satisfaction, because they are burdened by carrying the awful weight of the natural man—without any of the joys that come from progressing toward becoming "the man of Christ." They have scarcely "[begun] to be enlightened" (Alma 32:34). The meek and fully yoked, on the other hand, find God's reassuring grace and see their weakness yielding to strength (see Ether 12:27).

Strange as it seems, a few of the partially yoked, undeservedly wearing the colors of the kingdom, are just close enough to the prescribed path and process to be able to observe in others some of the visible costs of discipleship. Sobered by that observation, they want victory without battle and expect campaign ribbons merely for watching; but there is no witness until after the trial of their faith (see Ether 12:6).

These same Church members know just enough about the doctrines to converse superficially on them, but their scant knowledge about the deep doctrines is inadequate for deep discipleship (see 1 Corinthians 2:10). Thus uninformed about the deep doctrines, they make no deep change in their lives. They lack the faith to "give place" (Alma 32:27) consistently for real discipleship. Such members move out a few hundred yards from the entrance to the straight and narrow path and repose on the first little rise, thinking, "Well, this is all there is to it"; and they end up living far below their possibilities. While not as distant as those King Benjamin described — "For how knoweth a man the master whom he has not served, and who is a stranger unto him, and is far from the thoughts and intents of his heart?" (Mosiah 5:13) — these people are not drawing closer either.

Others are moving but, having pursued the wrong azimuth, find themselves caught in various cul-de-sacs. In order to resume the journey they must back up in full view of other climbers. These are among the moments when some find out whether they are "ashamed" of the gospel of Jesus Christ, including its grand principle of repentance.

Numerous valiant and faithful individuals are keeping their covenants and steadily developing the cardinal qualities of character necessary to become men and women of Christ. These enlightened ones meet adversity and overcome it; these have that special peace that overcomes even amid adversity. They also sustain the Brethren while knowing that the Brethren too are mortals. Such faithful know by the power of the Holy Ghost that Jesus is the Christ and that He was crucified for the sins of the world, enabling still others to believe on their words, which is sufficient for now (see D&C 46:13, 14).

The almost valiant resemble the valiant, except that they show considerably less consecration and measurably more murmuring. They are less settled spiritually and are more distracted by the world. They progress, but do so episodically rather than steadily and pause on plateaus.

A few in the Church are needlessly laden with programmed hyperactivity. They unwisely and unnecessarily exceed their strength and means, running faster than they are able (see D&C 10:4; Mosiah 4:27). Their fatiguing, Martha-like anxiety should yield more often to a Mary-like sense of proportion about what matters most; then the good part will not be taken from them (see Luke 10:41–42).

Much more burdening than that avoidable fatigue, however, is the burden of personal frailties. Almost all of us as members fail to lighten our load for the long and arduous journey of discipleship. We fail to put off the childish things

—not the tinker toys, but the temper tantrums; not training pants, but pride. We remain unnecessarily burdened by things which clearly should and can be jettisoned. No wonder some are weary and faint in their minds (see Hebrews 12:3).

Some members maintain only cultural ties to the Church. Often these people have had valiant parents but they themselves live off the fruits of discipleship banked by those parents and grandparents. They make no fresh, spiritual investments; they have neither new earnings nor an inheritance to pass along to their own posterity.

Then there are the dissenters who leave the Church, either formally or informally, but who cannot leave it alone. Usually anxious to please worldly galleries, they are critical or at least condescending towards the Brethren. They not only seek to steady the ark but also on occasion give it a hard shove! Often having been taught the same true doctrines as the faithful, they have nevertheless moved in the direction of dissent (see Alma 47:36). They have minds hardened by pride (see Daniel 5:20).

For these, would that the wisdom of King Benjamin were more operational! "Believe in God; believe that he is, and that he created all things, both in heaven and in earth; believe that he has all wisdom, and all power, both in heaven and in earth; believe that man doth not comprehend all the things which the Lord can comprehend" (Mosiah 4:9).

So it is that the challenges of becoming spiritually enlightened confront a varied constituency even in the Church. In addition, Church members live in a cultural context which, in itself, reflects varied views about the Christian faith. The seeming repetitiousness of life, for example, is seen by some in the world as its lack of purposefulness. Others translate their personal failures and frustrations into a conclusion that life reflects a total absence of meaning. Still others regard as proof of His nonexistence God's failure to perform according to their terms; the irony here being that they insist on God's compliance with their demands for proof, even though they are out of compliance with Him.

Some want to be free to choose, but to have God ever poised to rescue them. They want to call on God in their extremities, but don't want Him to interfere with their sensualities. They demand an undemanding God. Others want moral agency for humanity, but without the possibility of human misery. They desire permissiveness without the consequences of permissiveness.

No wonder we have so many words of counsel from the Savior and His prophets about the danger of our being "choked with the cares . . . and pleasures of this life" (Luke 8:14).

The scriptures note candidly that we can look around us and see "the ungodly . . . prosper in the world" (Psalm 73:12). Some conclude "it is vain to serve God" (Malachi 3:14). Truly, as Jesus said, "the world loves its own" and maintains its own system of rewards (see John 15:19). Scriptures counsel us, however, "that the triumphing of the wicked is short, and the joy of the hypocrite but for a moment" (Job 20:5).

Nevertheless the conditioning of the world is fierce and unremitting. Its conventional wisdom and prevailing patterns of life-style are saturatingly portrayed in music, film, literature, and so forth. To compound the problem, there really are vexing "evils and designs which do and will exist in the hearts of conspiring men in the last days" (D&C 89:4). This conspiracy plays to the cupidity and sensuality of the natural man, making it easier for some people to succumb by having their hearts "set . . . upon the things of this world" (D&C 121:35).

All this takes its toll. Nevertheless disciples can still live in the world but not be of it (see John 17:14). This means that our hearts must not become "overcharged with . . . the cares of this life" (Luke 21:34), blurring our vision:

> Having the understanding darkened, being alienated from the life of God through the ignorance that is in them, because of the blindness of their heart (Ephesians 4:18).

But if our gospel be hid, it is hid to them that are lost:

In whom the god of this world hath blinded the minds of them which believe not, lest the light of the glorious gospel of Christ, who is the image of God, should shine unto them (2 Corinthians 4:3–4).

No wonder that to some "the light of the glorious gospel" does not seem to shine brightly. Even the Light of the world shined in the darkness and the darkness comprehended Him not (see John 1:5).

Those enlightened ones who become the children of light are thenceforth not to be aligned with those of the world who are "alienated from the life of God." We are to put off the old man and put on the new man, the man of Christ. As we do this, we will "be kind to one another, tenderhearted, forgiving." (See Ephesians 4:17–32.) It is these latter experiences that so many mortals seldom have, and thus in their deprivation they become hardened.

Even while we move along the prescribed path, success itself is dangerous unless it is managed by meekness. For instance, when with divine help we participate in giving crucial aid, perhaps causing the small equivalent of a little gushing of living water from the barren rocks, we, like Moses, need to be careful about causality by avoiding what might be called the pronoun problem (see Numbers 20:10).

Our outward involvement in spiritual things can also be illusive. One can be present at sacrament meeting but not really worship; the physical body can be there, while the mind and heart are elsewhere. One can accept a calling but still not magnify it, ending up by simply serving time. One can pay fast offerings unaccompanied by any personal service to needy neighbors or to the poor. We can open our checkbooks in the same way as some open their scriptures —more in mechanical than spiritual compliance.

In church we can join in singing the hymns while being without a song in our hearts. We can take the sacrament with hand and mouth yet not be taken in mind, at least sometimes, to Gethsemane and Calvary. We can play artful doctrinal ping-pong in various Church classes but with minds and hearts that are less stretched than the ping-pong net.

Even more serious, a person can even go through the temple without letting it pass through him!

The superficial, public observance of Church callings and duties does not transform private lives. Since they are seemingly doing everything, however, the untransformed wonder why they do not have more spiritual satisfaction.

Even the faithful need to ponder their progress along the way. They may well consider these questions:

— If we halted less often to circle our wagons wearily or defensively, what more would God show and tell us about the far horizons in His "one eternal round"? (D&C 3:2.)

— If we were more willing to bear a larger yoke, how much more might we then learn of Him? (Matthew 11:29.)

— If we were more brave, where might we be sent to the rescue—not only of one soul, but of a whole, beleaguered battalion? (D&C 18:16.)

— If we would further strip ourselves of our jealousies and fears, what mountains of misunderstanding might we then move? (D&C 67:10.)

— If we could give up the pride-drenched portions of our self-image, how much might God accelerate our preparations for that far, far better world that the meek shall inherit? (D&C 121:37; Luke 9:62; Philippians 3:13–14.)

When we fall short, as we all do, God nevertheless encourages us, saying that His gifts are for those who keep his commandments "and him that seeketh so to do" (D&C 46:9).

For those athirst for the living waters, searching the holy scriptures will cause those books to release their nourishing juices and will invigorate us for the long journey of discipleship. Since we are instructed, "continue in patience until

ye are perfected" (D&C 67:13), such continuing nourishment
is vital.

Though merciful, God has set strict and clear conditions
for our returning to His presence. One of these conditions is
that we are to become enlightened as little children—in the
best spiritual sense of the word. There is a difference between
childishness and meek, perceptive childlikeness. In childishness there is a profound possessiveness: "That's my toy!"
There is open striving to be favored and ascendant: "That's
my place!" Unchecked, these and other tendencies—unabated in the child—soon harden into the natural man, who
is "an enemy to God" (Mosiah 3:19). The natural man is actually at cross purposes with God's plans. The natural man
really has different ends, seeks different outcomes, marches
to different drummers. If unrepentant, such become "carnal
and devilish, and the devil has power over them" (Mosiah
16:3).

Even though the natural man is his enemy, however, God
loves man:

> He doeth not anything save it be for the benefit of the
> world; for he loveth the world, even that he layeth down
> his own life that he may draw all men unto him. Wherefore,
> he commandeth none that they shall not partake of his
> salvation. (2 Nephi 26:24.)

> For he is our God; and we are the people of his pasture,
> and the sheep of his hand. To day if ye will hear his voice,
> harden not your heart. (Psalm 95:7–8.)

The challenge is to "put off the natural man," and "come
off conqueror" (Mosiah 3:19; D&C 10:5).

A prominent feature of the natural man is selfishness—
the inordinate and excessive concern with self. Prophets frequently warn about the dangers of this sin. The distance between constant self-pleasing and self-worship is shorter than
we think. Stubborn selfishness is actually rebellion against

God, because, warned Samuel, "stubbornness is as . . . idolatry" (1 Samuel 15:23).

Selfishness is much more than an ordinary problem, because it activates all the cardinal sins. It is the detonator in the breaking of the Ten Commandments.

By focusing on himself a person finds it naturally easier to bear false witness if it serves his purpose. It is easier to ignore his parents instead of honoring them. It is easier to steal, because what he wants prevails. It is easier to covet, since the selfish conclude that nothing should be denied them.

It is easier for the selfish person to commit sexual sins, because to please himself is the name of that deadly game in which others are often cruelly used. He easily neglects the Sabbath day, since one day soon becomes just like another. For the selfish it is easier to lie, because the truth is conveniently subordinated.

The selfish individual thus seeks to please not God but himself. He will even break a covenant in order to satisfy an appetite.

Selfishness has little time to regard seriously the sufferings of others, hence the love of many waxes cold (see Moses 6:27; Matthew 24:12; D&C 45:27).

Long ago it was prophesied that the last days would be rampant with selfishness and the other cardinal sins, just as in the days of Noah (see Matthew 24:37–39; 2 Timothy 3:1–5). Society in the days of Noah, scriptures advise, was "corrupt before God" and "filled with violence" (Genesis 6:11–12; Moses 8:28). Corruption and violence—does that sound familiar? Both of these awful conditions crest today because of surging individual selfishness. When thus engulfed, no wonder mens' hearts in our day will fail them because of fear (see Luke 21:26; D&C 45:26). Even the faithful can expect a few fibrillations.

Some selfishness exists even in good people. Jane Austen's character Elizabeth mused, "I have been a selfish being all my life, in practice, though not in principle" (*Pride and Prejudice* [New York: Airmont Books, 1962], p. 58). The selfish individual has a passion for the vertical pronoun *I*. It is interesting that the vertical pronoun *I* does not have knees to bend, while the first letter in the pronoun *we* does.

Selfishness, in its preoccupation with self, withholds from others deserved and needed praise, thereby causing a deprivation instead of giving a commendation.

We see in ourselves other familiar forms of selfishness: accepting or claiming undeserved credit; puffing deserved credit; being glad when others go wrong; resenting the genuine successes of others; preferring public vindication to private reconciliation; and taking "advantage of one because of his words" (2 Nephi 28:8). Such a person views all things selfishly — "What are their implications for me?" This is much like the traffic delay caused by the mattress on the highway. When each frustrated motorist finally got around the mattress none stopped to remove it, because now there was nothing in it for him.

The Prophet Joseph Smith declared, "Mankind [is] naturally selfish, ambitious, and striving to excel one above another" (*The Words of Joseph Smith*, comp. Andrew F. Ehat and Lyndon W. Cook [Provo, Utah: Brigham Young University, Religious Studies Center, 1980], p. 201). Saul, swollen with selfishness, may be taken as an example. The Lord reminded him about an earlier time "when thou wast little in thine own sight" (1 Samuel 15:17).

Selfishness is often expressed in stubbornness of mind. Having a "mind hardened in pride" (Daniel 5:20) often afflicts the brightest, who could also be the best. "One thing" the brightest often lack: meekness! Instead of having "a willing mind" which seeks to emulate the "mind of Christ," a mind hardened in pride is impervious to counsel and often seeks ascendancy (1 Chronicles 28:9; 1 Corinthians 2:16; D&C 64:34). Jesus, who was and is "more intelligent than they all" (Abraham 3:19), is also more meek than they all.

Jesus put everything on the altar without fanfare or bargaining. Both before and after His astonishing atonement He declared, "Glory be to the Father" (D&C 19:19; Moses 4:2). Jesus, though stunningly brilliant, allowed His will to be "swallowed up in the will of the Father" (Mosiah 15:7; see also John 6:38). Those with pride-hardened minds are simply unable to do this.

Stubborn selfishness leads otherwise good people to fight over herds, patches of sand, and strippings of milk. All this results from what the Lord calls coveting "the drop," while neglecting the "more weighty matters" (D&C 117:8). Myopic selfishness magnifies a mess of pottage and makes thirty pieces of silver look like a treasure trove. In our intense acquisitiveness we forget Him who once said, "What is property unto me?" (D&C 117:4.)

Such is the scope of putting off the burdensome natural man (see Mosiah 3:19), who is naturally selfish. So much of our fatigue in fact comes from carrying that needless load. This heaviness of the natural man prevents us from doing our Christian calisthenics; so we end up too swollen with selfishness to pass through the narrow needle's eye.

Anne Morrow Lindbergh wrote of the need to "shed my Martha-like anxiety about many things, . . . shedding pride, . . . shedding hypocrisy in human relationships. What a rest that will be! The most exhausting thing in life, I have discovered, is being insincere. That is why so much of social life is exhausting." (*Gift from the Sea* [New York: Vintage Books, 1978], p. 32.)

Unchecked selfishness thus stubbornly blocks the way for developing all of the divine qualities: love, mercy, patience, long-suffering, kindness, graciousness, goodness, and gentleness. Any tender sprouts from these virtues are sheared off by sharp selfishness. In contrast, there is not a single gospel covenant the keeping of which does not shear off selfishness from us!

But what a battle for some of us! We are all afflicted in different degrees. The question is, How goes the battle? Is our selfishness being put off—even if only gradually? Or is the natural man like the man who came to dinner? Divine tutoring is given largely in order to help us shed our selfishness, "for what son [or daughter] is [there] whom the father chasteneth not?" (Hebrews 12:7.)

Restoration scriptures tell us much about how we can really be forgiven through the atonement of Christ, by means of which, finally, "mercy . . . overpowereth justice" (Alma 34:15). We can have real and justified hope for the future—enough hope to develop the faith necessary to both put off the natural man and to strive to become more saintly.

Furthermore, because the centerpiece of the Atonement is already in place, we know that everything else in God's plan will likewise finally succeed. God is surely able to do His own work (see 2 Nephi 27:20–21). In His plans for the human family, long ago God made ample provision for all mortal mistakes. His purposes will all triumph, and will do so without abrogating man's moral agency. Moreover, all His purposes will come to pass in their time (see D&C 64:32).

Without these and other spiritual perspectives, it is instructive to see how differently we behave. Take away an acknowledgment of divine design and then watch the selfish scurrying to redesign political and economic systems to make life pain-free and pleasure-filled. (Misguided governments mean to live, even if they live beyond their means, thereby mortgaging future generations.)

Take away regard for the divinity in our neighbor, and note the decline in our regard for his property.

Take away basic moral standards, and observe how quickly tolerance changes into permissiveness.

Take away the sacred sense of belonging to a family or community, and notice how quickly citizens cease to care for big cities.

Take away regard for the seventh commandment, and behold the current celebration of sex, the secular religion, with its own liturgy of lust and supporting music. Its theology focuses on self. Its hereafter is now. Its chief ritual is sensation—though the irony is that it finally desensitizes its obsessed adherents, who become "past feeling" (Ephesians 4:19; Moroni 9:20).

Thus, in all its various expressions, selfishness is really self-destruction in slow motion.

Each spasm of selfishness narrows the universe that much more by shutting down our awareness of others and by making us more and more alone. We then desperately seek sensations precisely in order to verify that one really exists. A variation occurs when we are full of self-pity over affectional deprivation and we end up in serious transgression.

Surging selfishness presents us with a sobering scene as the natural man acts out his wants. Many assert their needs —but where have we lodged the corresponding obligations? So many have become demanders, but where are all the providers? There are many more people with things to say than there are listeners. There are more neglected and aging parents than there are attentive sons and daughters— though, numerically, clearly it should not be so.

Just as Jesus warned that some evil spirits would not *come out* except by "prayer and fasting" (Matthew 17:21), so the natural man does not *come off* without difficulty, either.

As regards this personal battle, the Lord has urged us to so live that we will "come off conqueror" (D&C 10:5). But we cannot come off conqueror except we first "put off" the selfish, natural man.

The natural man is truly God's enemy, because the natural man will keep God's precious children from true and everlasting happiness. Our full happiness requires our becoming the man or woman of Christ.

The meek men and women of Christ are quick to praise but are also able to restrain themselves. They understand that on occasion the biting of the tongue can be as important as the gift of tongues.

The man and woman of Christ are easily entreated, but the selfish person is not. Christ never brushed aside those in need because He had bigger things to do. Furthermore, the men and women of Christ are constant, being the same in private as in public. We cannot keep two sets of books while heaven has but one.

The men and women of Christ magnify their callings without magnifying themselves. Whereas the natural man says "Worship me" and "Give me thy power," the men and women of Christ seek to exercise power by long-suffering and by unfeigned love (see Moses 1:12; 4:3; D&C 121:41).

Whereas the natural man vents his anger, the men and women of Christ are "not easily provoked" (1 Corinthians 13:5). Whereas the natural man is filled with greed, the men and women of Christ "seeketh not [their] own" (1 Corinthians 13:5). Whereas the natural man seldom denies himself worldly pleasures, the men and women of Christ seek to bridle all their passions (see Alma 38:12).

Whereas the natural man covets praise and riches, the men and women of Christ know that such things are but the "drop" (D&C 117:8). Human history's happiest irony will be that the covenant-keeping, unselfish individuals will finally receive "all that [the] Father hath"! (D&C 84:38.)

One of the last, subtle strongholds of selfishness is the natural feeling that we "own" ourselves. Of course, we are free to choose and are personally accountable. Yes, we have individuality. But those who have chosen to "come unto Christ" soon realize that they do not "own" themselves. Instead, they belong to Him! We are to become consecrated along with our gifts, our appointed days, and our very selves. Hence there is a stark difference between stubbornly "owning" oneself and submissively belonging to God. Clinging to the old self is a mark not of independence but of indulgence.

The Prophet Joseph promised that when selfishness is annihilated, we "may comprehend all things, present, past, and future" (*The Personal Writings of Joseph Smith,* comp. Dean C. Jesse [Salt Lake City: Deseret Book Co., 1984], p. 485). Even now, however, in gospel glimpses we can see things "as they really are" (Jacob 4:13).

Indeed, the gospel brings glorious illumination as to our possibilities. Scales fall from our eyes with the shedding of selfishness. Then we begin to see our luminous and true identity.

Given the sobering and almost intimidating size of the challenge, what else is there to help us?

The significant words directed by the Lord through the Apostle Paul tell us why Christ established the Church with its foundation of apostles and prophets, with Jesus Christ Himself as the chief cornerstone (Ephesians 2:20). The Church was established "for the perfecting of the saints," the very process of our becoming men and women of Christ. The Church is established "for the work of the ministry" and for the "edifying of the body of Christ," the members of the Church. This was necessary too in order for us to have a "unity of the faith" and also "of the knowledge of the son of God." In addition we are urged to strive to progress "unto a perfect man, unto the measure of the stature of the fulness of Christ." (Ephesians 4:12–13.)

Without the Church and its Apostles and prophets we could, in fact, be severely "tossed to and fro," being "carried about with every wind of doctrine." We could be manipulated "by the sleight of men" and their conspiracies and cunning craftiness (Ephesians 4:14).

True Christianity thus requires real authority, real verity, real orthodoxy, and real unity! Then let the storms and the winds come, including the various "winds of doctrine."

Conventional wisdom already advises humanity that, if they want to, individuals can have sexual relations outside of legal heterosexual marriage; they can have freedom without responsibility; they have entitlements without work. Conventional wisdom likewise declares we cannot know that which is to come (see Jacob 7:7). Therefore, it concludes, seek present pleasure and avoid present pain.

The scriptures frequently decry yielding to the persuasions of men; also, fearing men more than God (D&C 3:7; 5:21). The presence of prophets and Apostles encourages and helps the flock to resist this temptation.

While the Church has been established in our time never to be disestablished, all the risks are still there for individual Church members. The life-styles and teachings of the world can still overcome those individuals who allow themselves to be tossed "to and fro," who are unanchored in the teachings of Jesus and will not receive direction from His Apostles and prophets.

The unity we are to achieve must be that special unity that reflects the "mind of Christ" (1 Corinthians 2:16). We are not, said Paul, to be children in understanding, but rather to be men (see 1 Corinthians 14:20). Indeed, men of Christ!

After describing the significance and essential features of the Church, Paul urged its members to go forward, "speaking the truth in love," urging them to "grow up into him in all things, . . . even Christ" (Ephesians 4:15).

The Apostles and prophets were not to preside over a debating society or some loose intellectual confederacy, but rather over a kingdom. They are to see to it that there is a unity in the Church that is edifying. The "edifying" of the Church includes giving encouragement, supplying needed correction, and providing the ordinances and the covenants, including those of the holy temple. To edify means to instruct, benefit, or uplift—to uplift morally and spiritually, to give important moral guidance.

The Church strives to help members "come to the knowledge of the Son of God, unto a perfect man" (JST, Ephesians 4:13), which is the theme of this volume.

What we should really feel threatened by is not that spiritual change but such things as our failure to use our many opportunities for service, being overcome by the world, being passively engaged in good causes, and breaking our covenants. So often, when seemingly threatened, we tend to move all our guns to the starboard, where there is actually no real assault, leaving unguarded the port side, where the barbarians clamber aboard unhindered.

Daily life casts up many examples of our common need to develop the uncommon virtues. A person can overreact to incursions into his "territory"—his status, property, role, and so on; can feel unappreciated, not understood, left out, unlistened to; can feel beset, overwhelmed, weary; can feel pain—physical and emotional. Moreover, these are not always merely feelings; sometimes they are harsh realities. Roles are threatened and altered; property is stolen or altered; people are ignored; and pain is certainly part of the human experience.

But being broken economically, though devastating, is not as serious as broken covenants. Alteration or even loss of a professional role does not obliterate one's role as a child of God. Being overlooked or being left out of a local "inner circle" does not alter the reality of our belonging to God eternally.

Why is it all so hard? Because we live in the here and now, and because the world is, in fact, "too much with us." The rewards of eternity seem remote when compared to being snubbed just a moment ago or being passed over for a promotion last week. Furthermore, when we fail by some mortal measure we worry, especially since such measures seem to be the only ones visibly operative. So why shouldn't we notice? Indeed, how can we fail to notice?

Yet the scriptures give reassuring examples of those who noticed but who exercised eternal perspective amid mortal pressures. For instance, Adam and Eve taught and shared "all things" with their children (Moses 5:12). These wonderful parents must have experienced deep disappointment over Cain and his posterity as the centuries passed. Happy as Adam doubtless was at the time of the gathering of his and Eve's righteous posterity at Adam-ondi-Ahman, many of their descendants were not there (D&C 107:53). As parents, Adam and Eve had taught well, but they had been unlistened to by Cain and others of their children, whose posterity along with ours are "free to choose" (2 Nephi 2:27).

In the midst of all of his afflictions in what was a veritable deluge of suffering, submissive Job refused to rail against God or to "charge God foolishly" (Job 1:22). Though he suffered loss of health, wealth, loved ones, and more, combined with his being mocked for his faith, Job clung to the eternal verities, such as the reality of the resurrection. He did not pretend to understand the why of it all. Like perplexed Nephi (see 1 Nephi 11:17), he did not know the meaning of all things but he knew that God loved him!

If we understand eternal verities, then we can at least put the mortal perplexities and complexities in their perspective. Though we will still experience these perplexities and complexities in unabated force, the strong but supple framework of faith will help to absorb them.

Life's tactical choices actually present the opportunity to exercise our moral agency. Such constitute the calisthenics of choice. The chief impediment, however, is our lack of full spiritual alignment. For instance, we have our hand to the plow, but we are looking back. We have turned away from evil, but we have not yet turned fully to God. We proceed with implementation, but do so only with hesitation—as when a decision involves how much time we are willing to spend nurturing a neighbor in need and our decision may be to delay or to nurture only occasionally.

Will we really feast on the word of God or merely nibble? If a person's particular struggle is to become more patient, will his efforts tend to be episodic, displaying hesitation rather than consecration?

Lives like these are essentially good lives—decent, free of serious transgression—but are still not "valiant in the testimony of Jesus" (D&C 76:79). Do we remember, "one thing thou lackest" (Mark 10:21)? The Master has said "Come, follow me." Jesus' arm of mercy is extended all the day long (Jacob 5:47; 6:5; Mosiah 29:20). He waits for us with open arms (Mormon 6:17). He has set the pattern, given the example, and shown us the straightness and narrowness of the way, including how "by strict obedience" he prevailed and overcame the world. It can be no different for us.

Many marvelous things have been given to us! To quote King Benjamin, the task is "now if ye believe . . . these things see that ye do them" (Mosiah 4:10). To that end, summational statements by the prophets are quite direct and simple. "Continue in the way which is narrow. . . . What can I say more?" (Jacob 6:11–12.) "Ye know the things that ye must do" (3 Nephi 27:21). "The Holy Ghost . . . will show unto you all things what ye should do" (2 Nephi 32:5).

So it is and so it will be with one who is enlightened enough to strive to become a man or woman of Christ.

CHAPTER 2

"Enlightened by the Spirit of Truth"

Those who are "enlightened by the Spirit of truth" (D&C 6:15) and who continue faithful are those whom the Lord will lead "in a strait and narrow course across that everlasting gulf of misery" and "land their . . . immortal souls at the right hand of God" (Helaman 3:29–30). One thing is certain: there is no "natural man . . . that knoweth" (Alma 26:20–21) about this special journey.

To begin with, the journey must not seem so intimidating that it remains unattempted! In the Greek from which it was translated, the term *perfect* in Matthew 5:48 of our Bible means "fully developed," to become "finished" as to our individual potential and to have "completed" the course God has set forth for us to follow (see Matthew 5:48, LDS Edition of the Bible, page 1195, footnote 48b). All of the godly attributes, to the degree developed through our "diligence and obedience," will actually rise with us in the resurrection, giving us "so much the advantage in the world to come" (D&C 130:19). After we leave this life there will be no sudden setting apart that will, for instance, make us instantly perfect in the attribute of patience. Instead, we are to "work out" this dimension of our exaltation now and subsequently. Hence it is best to aim for steady progression rather than to be intimidated and immobilized by the concept of being perfect or "finished or completed." We should display diligent discipleship but not expect it all to happen either at once or easily.

In this connection, my frustrated golfing friends once urged me to improve my poor putting by imagining around the cup concentric circles with diameters of two or six or even eight feet — "Just get closer!" We can liken this to our discipleship as we strive to "get closer" to each specific characteristic of Christ.

Whenever one holds up the demanding standards of the gospel, even in such a simplified way as the putting analogy, some may still worry about whether just aspiring to develop spiritually adds inordinate stress to life. In this important matter, many scriptures help us to be "enlightened by the Spirit of truth."

Certainly there can be no moderation as regards keeping the seventh commandment, "Thou shalt not commit adultery" (Exodus 20:14). There can be no relief from gospel requirements in which abstinence rather than moderation is the commandment. But in any case individuals are most severely stressed by sin. It constitutes the greatest burden, other burdens and other stresses being small by comparison. And this stress is removable!

The stress most faithful Church members feel arises out of the shared pressures of daily life, the temptations and afflictions common to mortals. These real pressures are unnecessarily increased when some unwisely place upon themselves unrealistic expectations. As to this avoidable stress, the Lord's instructions are very clear:

Do not run faster or labor more than you have strength and means provided to enable you to translate; but be diligent unto the end (D&C 10:4).

And see that all these things are done in wisdom and order; for it is not requisite that a man should run faster than he has strength. And again, it is expedient that he should be diligent, that thereby he might win the prize; therefore, all things must be done in order. (Mosiah 4:27.)

Paced progress not only is acceptable to the Lord but also is recommended by Him. Divine declarations say: "Ye are little children and ye cannot bear all things now" (D&C 50:40); "I will lead you along" (D&C 78:18). Just as divine disclosure usually occurs line upon line, precept upon precept, here a little and there a little, so likewise we will achieve our spiritual progress gradually (see D&C 128:21; 98:12).

Rather than seeing ourselves as failing simply because we do not become immediately perfect, such as in the attribute of mercy, we should seek to become ever more merciful "in process of time." Even amid diligence, there need not be unrealistic expectations. Though imperfect, an improving person can actually know that the course of his life is generally acceptable to the Lord despite there being much distance yet to be covered. (See LDS Bible Dictionary, "Faith," pp. 669–70.)

Many modest people are actually further along than they realize in developing certain of the key Christian virtues. Having first of all brought with them some important "luggage," representing their earlier progress in the premortal world, they are "added upon." As they make still further progress here and now, this will give them much-needed inner satisfaction and confidence. This quiet reassurance can help to temper the outer stress arising from other roles and circumstances in life. A further stress-reducer is that as we become more merciful and long-suffering we will be less badgered by disappointments over the failures of others. As we become more patient, life, though still demanding, will be less hectic.

If we are keeping our covenants and progressing, though gradually, in the cardinal attributes, this is what matters most! Other things matter much, much less! A simple, settled focus on keeping covenants and on developing the cardinal characteristics can do much to provide proper perspective about the "weightier matters." The cardinal qualities, though unevenly developed, will also bring an added measure of spiritual poise.

These qualities constitute a community of interactive attributes that support each other. They give us greater strength to overcome the lust, pride, grief, and selfishness, tendencies that, if unevicted, especially fatigue us. These negative drives not only put us "on the rack" but if unchecked can also turn into obsessions, making us "like the troubled sea, when it cannot rest. . . . There is no peace . . . to the wicked." (Isaiah 57:20–21.)

Spiritual synergy is therefore a treasured and promised blessing of discipleship. If we keep our covenants, serve others (both in our callings and otherwise), worship, study, and pray, at the same time we are quietly hastening our spiritual development of the cardinal virtues.

Some cautions are in order, however. While we should be "anxiously engaged," we need not be hectically engaged. We can be diligent and still do things in "wisdom and order" —without going faster than we "have strength and means" (Mosiah 4:27; D&C 10:4).

The costs of discipleship are nevertheless real. They can be paid neither at wholesale rates nor in one lump sum:

> And whosoever doth not bear his cross, and come after me, cannot be my disciple.
>
> For which of you, intending to build a tower, sitteth not down first, and counteth the cost, whether he have sufficient to finish it?
>
> Lest haply, after he hath laid the foundation, and is not able to finish it, all that behold it begin to mock him,

Saying, This man began to build, and was not able to finish.

Or what king, going to make war against another king, sitteth not down first, and consulteth whether he be able with ten thousand to meet him that cometh against him with twenty thousand?

Or else, while the other is yet a great way off, he sendeth an ambassage, and desireth conditions of peace.

So likewise, whosoever he be of you that forsaketh not all that he hath, he cannot be my disciple. (Luke 14:27–33.)

While we cannot expect discipleship to be cost free, we can receive God's helping grace, including compensatory blessings, along with inner joy over what is jettisoned in putting off the natural man. Thereby we can, for instance, end the gnawing stress of being unsettled: "Wherefore, settle this in your hearts, that ye will do the things which I shall teach, and command you" (JST, Luke 14:28).

We can ease the stress induced by our inconsistency, pain through which we put ourselves repeatedly. Unfortunately, like Oliver Cowdery, we do not always "continue as [we] commenced" (D&C 9:5). As with our wasteful automobile driving habits that consume extra energy because of quick starts and stops, so it may be that with inconsistent discipleship we actually inflict costs on ourselves in the face of divine counsel.

Lowered self-esteem results from such needless exhaustion. The enthusiasm of "I'll baptize a thousand on my mission!" is best tempered by "I'll go where you want me to go, dear Lord . . . I'll do what you want me to do," letting "God give the increase" (*Hymns*, no. 270; 1 Corinthians 3:6).

We can be overwrought by seeking the praise and honors of the world. Such individuals are "anxiously engaged" in putting points on a local scoreboard. Heavy stress occurs in gaining the whole world while losing our souls (see Mark 8:36).

We can also end the genuine stress which goes with unrepented-of sin by pleading, "More holiness give me," and by receiving the "peace . . . which passeth all understanding" (*Hymns*, no. 131; John 14:27; Philippians 4:7).

We can likewise diminish (at least our portion of) the painful stress that accompanies unresolved interpersonal differences: "Moreover if thy brother shall trespass against thee, go and tell him his fault between thee and him alone: if he shall hear thee, thou hast gained thy brother" (Matthew 18:15).

We can end the exhausting stress that goes with jealousies and fears (see D&C 67:10).

We can end the subtle but awful stress of resisting conscience (see Mosiah 4:3).

We can dissolve the stress of wearily listening to "so many kinds of voices in the world" (1 Corinthians 14:10). A true disciple need tune in on only one channel: "My sheep hear my voice" (John 10:27). Like ancient Athenians, some today spend their energies and "their time in nothing else, but either to tell, or to hear some new thing" (Acts 17:21). A true disciple will not listen to the voices that deny the divinity of Jesus or of His latter-day work, that deny the apostolic foundations of the Restoration, or that suggest compromising with the world.

So it is that we can end much stress in life, if we will. Genuine discipleship is a way of shedding the sources of stress discussed above.

Neither need we experience overwrought anxiety concerning our weaknesses. Such fretting can become a substitute for doing something about them. Nor should we let a mistake or a disappointment mire us in self-pity.

On the other hand, we should not be passively or defensively self-contented by constantly excusing ourselves rather than earnestly proving ourselves. Rather than being an intimidation, the very act of noticing our failures and our weaknesses can be an invitation, an invitation to overcome them patiently and "in process of time."

Meanwhile there are more opportunities for service all around us, lying conveniently within our individual circles of influence—more than we ever use. Rendering service not only helps others but gets our minds off ourselves, putting our own problems in perspective.

Reflection too is required in order to assimilate all of our on-rushing experiences. Unless the lessons from our past are humbly harvested, our storehouses of memory will contain too few relevant remembrances. Patience facilitates such pondering and reflecting. Pondering sorts things out, rearranging some of the furniture of the mind while giving place for new furnishings.

Faith hastens repentance. Faith induces the quiet scrubbing of the soul that is part of our being anxiously engaged. Spiritual housework is done room by room and corner by corner. In some seasons of our lives, this is supplemented by inspirationally induced bursts of spring cleaning. Even so, we are to do our spiritual housework in wisdom and order, without trying to run faster than we have strength and means provided (see Mosiah 4:27; D&C 10:4).

After all, real repentance consists of *turning away* from that which is wrong and also *turning to* God. A full revolution! This is the most lasting and beneficial of all revolutions!

In contrast, those in an uncompleted process of repentance are stranded. In this circumstance their inadequacies are highlighted cruelly and repeatedly, because their ambivalence prevents a full revolution. By turning fully to God, however, they receive His helping graces, including the needed reinforcing spiritual experiences. (See Alma 32.)

But even when that full revolution has been made, in self-improvement there is a straight and narrow path. A wise pace is vital here too, for we are at risk if we slip off either side. On one side is the precipice of fretful anxiety and guilt; on the other, steep self-contentment. To run faster than we are able is dangerous. So are dawdling, looking back, and zigging and zagging.

Similarly, being deeply discouraged makes the trail risky. Often we tally our failures with great precision and self-depreciating fanfare while failing to inwardly record our successes. For instance, after a disappointing personal act of expressing our ego we may exclaim inwardly, "I have done it again!" Clearly, even God's long-suffering cannot excuse us; nevertheless He still waits for us to move from recognition on through to remission. "His arm is extended to all people who will repent" (Alma 19:36). He thereby provides fresh "space" and encouragement "all the day long" (2 Nephi 28:32). He is ever encouraging us to regroup and try again. And there are no restrictive office hours for receiving returning prodigals—night and day He awaits us!

It is worth noting too that, as regrettable as an act of impulsive ego can be, it may helpfully, though painfully, underscore our need for more meekness. Too much cleverness by half may finally and fortunately embarrass us sufficiently to cause us to develop more empathy. When at length we tire of putting people down, this self-inflicted fatigue can give way to the invigorating calisthenics of lifting people up.

If we are too eager to push ourselves forward, the sudden shame of such over-reaching can cause us to hold back at last. Harsh as the exposure of such a weakness can be and subduing as the self-realization of such shortfalls is, this circumstance can be a spur to improvement if we have the meekness and faith to repent; whereas if we had not been jarred sufficiently, perhaps the need to work on something we were lacking would have been obscured.

Improving does not always mean restraining, either. It can mean venturing, as with spiritual growth. Here the shy who need to venture can do so—but without expecting perfection in their early assertions; they will gain some needed experience along with some incremental improvement. On the other hand, if a person is impulsive but finally succeeds somewhat in holding back, he should rejoice but not think this is full humility all at once; however, he will still gain the needed experience of instructive waiting in the wings instead of occupying center stage. After all, when we learn to "shine as lights in the world" (Philippians 2:15) there is no need to be in the spotlight. Such lesser incandescence is of no interest.

If we have an irrepressible urge to manage things, this pattern can be made to yield to taking turns and also to profiting more from the leadership of others. Besides, the "take charge" mentality is out of alignment with the meekness of Jesus. The divine counsel "Be still, and know that I am God" (Psalm 46:10) is a required basic lesson not only in self-restraint but also in deference. "Stop, and stand still until I command thee, and I will provide means whereby thou mayest accomplish the thing which I have commanded thee" (D&C 5:34).

To play at being God, even in micro ways, is evidence of too little faith in Him and too much confidence in ourselves. Such presumptuousness clearly leaves us unprepared to live with God "in humble reverence . . . forever and ever" (D&C 67:93).

We must be meek even in our minor developmental successes. A difficult situation may have actually been resolved by the grace of God "after all we can do." To recognize this fact inwardly is good, but to confess it openly is even better.

After His moment of great personal triumph and of supernal service, when in supreme success Jesus had "descended below all things" and "below them all," in order to comprehend all things (D&C 88:6; 122:8), when He had "trodden the winepress alone" (D&C 76:107), He nevertheless said, "Glory be to the Father" (D&C 19:19). He claimed no glory for Himself.

By our giving the honor, praise, and glory to God, we are actually being intellectually honest; unprofitable servants had best not claim too much credit. Similarly, giving deserved credit to others not only enhances our graciousness but it also can help us to steer the narrow channel between the dangerous rocks of self-adulation and destructive self-criticism.

As we thus begin to sprout spiritually "in that thing" (Alma 32:34) — whatever quality we are experimenting upon — we accumulate our own reinforcing evidence, which reassures us that we are on the right path and helps to keep us there.

Of course, many other things are still left undone. But the process is under way, and we know it. When thus assured inwardly and spiritually, we need not go away sorrowing because of all we yet lack (see Luke 18:22–23).

Once having turned fully to the Lord, we are now more free to follow him—"I will go before your face. I will be on your right hand and on your left." (D&C 84:88.) This is just the guidance we need on the straight and narrow path. Things then unfold—"here a little, and there a little," "line upon line, precept upon precept," for we "cannot bear all things now" (D&C 128:21; 98:12; 50:40). And every step forward mercifully brings with it its own reinforcing.

This is all done, then, in process of time, as described by the Prophet Joseph Smith, who knew the process well:

> The nearer man approaches perfection, the clearer are his views, and the greater his enjoyments, till he has overcome the evils of his life and lost every desire for sin; and like the ancients, arrives at that point of faith where he is wrapped in the power and glory of his Maker and is caught up to dwell with Him. But we consider that this is a station to which no man ever arrived in a moment. (Joseph Fielding Smith, comp., *Teachings of the Prophet Joseph Smith* [Salt Lake City: Deseret Book Company, 1976], p. 51.)

It is understandable, therefore, that we encounter no instant Christians—only reasonably constant disciples.

As we strive to continue faithful we especially need God's help in our moments of disappointment. That is when we could lose our courage, our bearings, and whatever spiritual momentum we have gained. It is precisely when we have done something foolish that we most need direction from God's omniscience. When we are drenched in self-disappointment we most need the reminders of who we really are. When we have been unfair we need the reassurance of His perfect love and His ever-extended arm of mercy.

How marvelous our Father and Jesus Christ are![1] They are perfected in all their attributes, thus enabling us to place full confidence in them without reservation.

While the egoistic urge of the natural man is to invite others, "Look at me," instead we should increasingly say, "Look to God and live" (Alma 37:47). When our natural instinct is to claim credit, increasingly we should ponder what they have done for us—a rescuing which we mortals were absolutely powerless to effect for ourselves. No wonder we are comparatively "unprofitable servants" (Mosiah 2:21).

Though we are "unprofitable," however, the Lord has not said we are worthless. In fact, He has said the worth of each soul is great in His sight (D&C 18:13–15). But the vast differences between what He has done for us and what we do for Him truly make us comparatively unprofitable. Nevertheless we are His servants. More important, we are His children! And He is a perfect and nurturing Father.

That choice relationship gives us another one—spirit siblings everywhere. Of these, in the shared journey of discipleship we hope true friends will blow away the chaff of our mistakes. But we must also do some of this for ourselves while conserving the kernels.

Putting one's hand to the plow without looking back means turning firmly and resolutely away from the past and focusing one's energies on the future. By pressing forward we hasten any needed forgetting (see Philippians 3:13–14). Thus we obtain a fresh view instead of perpetually letting ourselves "droop in sin" by sagging intellectually or in courage (2 Nephi 4:28).

As to that portion of our past which is relevant and instructive, the Holy Ghost will bring things to our remem-

---

1. In praising the Father and the Son for their qualities, it should be said most emphatically that while we have much less information about the Holy Ghost, that special spiritual personage could not comfort us without Himself being marvelously developed as to all the key attributes.

brance. He will also comfort us, so that any remembrance can be redemptive in its effect rather than debilitating or discouraging. The Holy Ghost, as our meekness makes possible, is ever working to ensure that we are "in a preparation to hear the word" (Alma 32:6), including that portion of the word most relevant to our circumstances.

On the road to Damascus, Saul may have already been "in a preparation," perhaps brooding and pondering before his great vision. In fact, he was told that it was hard for him to kick against the goads (see Acts 9:5; 26:14). Then the Lord revealed Himself in His true identity — as Jesus! There could be no mistaking by Paul. Thereafter he had a healthy attitude: "forgetting those things which are behind . . . I press [forward]" (Philippians 3:13–14). We are likewise to press forward and continue faithful, having come this far by faith.

As we do so, not only will the Holy Ghost prompt us but also, if we will listen, there will be helpful Jethros in our lives too, encouraging us and saying, "You can do better!"

An ironical slant is that, while initially turned to God, if we are not meek we may be less patient with those who have the same unresolved weaknesses as we have. Oh, we know those symptoms so well! While any similarities should evoke more mercy and empathy from us, instead they may merely be irritating reminders. Since we have yet to take the full cure ourselves, the same symptoms in others may be provoking.

Other provocations too may occur. For instance, when we are in the process of improving, discouraging things will surely arise. The safe passage of a soul across the gulf of misery never occurs without his encountering some stormy seas. Our defects may even be openly cited by others, even though some genuine spiritual improvement is visibly under way.

But as real as the challenges are in putting off the natural man, doing so is necessary in order for us to become the children of Christ; and of such is the kingdom of heaven.

CHAPTER 3

"The Children of Christ"

A significant portion of King Benjamin's towering and enlightening sermon was given to him by an angel, and even angels speak by the power of the Holy Ghost (Mosiah 3:2; 2 Nephi 32:3). At the center of the sermon is the masterful declaration about the exclusive means of salvation: "There shall be no other name given nor any other way nor means whereby salvation can come unto the children of men, only in and through the name of Christ, the Lord Omnipotent" (Mosiah 3:17; see also Mosiah 4:7).

Once spiritually enlightened, the "children of men" can become "the children of Christ." The latter phrase is shown to be more than a vague goal, because our Savior has taught us specifically. Thus it is not only the divinity but also the specificity of King Benjamin's sermon that marks it as outstanding. Years later father Helaman, in sending his two sons, Lehi and Nephi, on a mission to the land of Nephi, exhorted them, "Remember, remember my sons the words which king Benjamin spake unto his people" (Helaman 5:9).

In Restoration scriptures, therefore, not only salvation is specific but so also is the identity of the Savior, as the various scriptures foretold. A Savior was to be provided in the meridian of time (Moses 5:57). His name was to be Jesus Christ (2 Nephi 25:19). Christ volunteered for that mission premortally (Abraham 3:27). He was to be born of Mary, in Bethlehem, a Nazarene, hence He would be known as a Nazarene; a matter over which some stumbled in the meridian of time.

> Many of the people therefore, when they heard this saying, said, Of a truth this is the Prophet.
>
> Others said, This is the Christ. But some said, Shall Christ come out of Galilee?
>
> Hath not the scripture said, That Christ cometh of the seed of David, and out of the town of Bethlehem, where David was?
>
> So there was a division among the people because of him. (John 7:40–43. See also Micah 5:2; Luke 2:4; Matthew 2:23; 1 Nephi 11:13; Alma 7:10.)

There would even be a new star celebrating His birth (Helaman 14:5; 3 Nephi 1:21).

The sacrifice of the Father's firstborn in the spirit, His Only Begotten Son in the flesh, was the sacrifice of a Creator-God. The Atoner was the Lord God Omnipotent, who created this and other planets (see D&C 76:24; Moses 1:33; Mosiah 3:5). Therefore, unlike any sacrifice a mortal could have made, Christ's was an "infinite atonement"; made possible, declared King Benjamin, by the infinite goodness and mercy of God and by His willingness to see His Son suffer and be slain (see Mosiah 4:6; 2 Nephi 9:7; Alma 34:10, 12; Mosiah 5:3).

Not only was the coming of the Mortal Messiah prophesied but also his being disregarded, and even crucified. Said Benjamin:

And lo, he cometh unto his own, that salvation might come unto the children of men even through faith on his name; and even after all this they shall consider him a man, . . . and shall scourge him, and shall crucify him (Mosiah 3:9).

And Nephi wrote:

And the world, because of their iniquity, shall judge him to be a thing of naught; wherefore they scourge him, and he suffereth it; and they smite him, and he suffereth it. Yea, they spit upon him, and he suffereth it, because of his loving kindness and his long-suffering towards the children of men. (1 Nephi 19:9.)

The denigrating of Jesus' divinity has, alas, continued in our time. C. S. Lewis wrote: "The sweetly-attractive human Jesus is a product of 19th century skepticism, produced by people who were ceasing to believe in His divinity but wanted to keep as much Christianity as they could" (*Letters of C. S. Lewis* [London: Geoffrey Bles, Ltd., 1966], p. 181).

Regardless of how mortals view Him, however, there is no other saving and atoning name under heaven (Mosiah 3:17; Moses 6:52). "O remember, remember, . . . that there is no other way nor means whereby man can be saved, only through the atoning blood of Jesus Christ, who shall come; yea, remember that he cometh to redeem the world" (Helaman 5:9). All other "gods" but Him will finally fail and fall, including all the "ism" gods of this world and the many secular Caesars who, as we see currently, continue to come and go in "an hour of pomp, an hour of show."

The Restoration scriptures constitute the affirmative answer to what Amulek called "the great question": Is there really a redeeming Christ? (See Alma 34:5.)

If it were not true, as Abinadi prophesied, that Christ would rise as the first fruits of the resurrection, with all mortals to follow, then life would end in hopelessness (see Mosiah 16:6–7). But He is risen, and because of that life has profound purpose and rich meaning, which include our striving to become like Him. One day, said King Benjamin, such knowledge of the Savior would spread "throughout every nation, kindred, tongue, and people" (Mosiah 3:20). This spreading is happening in our day. At a still later day the degree of divine disclosure will be total and remarkable: "The day cometh that . . . all things shall be revealed unto the children of men which ever have been among the children of men, and which ever will be even unto the end of the earth" (2 Nephi 27:11).

There will be much to disclose, since all the prophets have testified of the coming of Jesus Christ (Mosiah 13:33), and we do not yet have all their words. Jesus, the Lord of all the prophets, even called them all "my prophets" (3 Nephi 1:13). Then how could He, as some aver, merely be one of them? Worse still, some consider Jesus only as another "moral teacher." In contrast, repeated pronouncements such as Abinadi's underscore Jesus' transcending triumph:

> And thus God breaketh the bands of death, having gained the victory over death; giving the Son power to make intercession for the children of men—
> Having ascended into heaven, having the bowels of mercy; being filled with compassion towards the children of men; standing betwixt them and justice; having broken the bands of death, taken upon himself their iniquity and their transgressions, having redeemed them, and satisfied the demands of justice (Mosiah 15:8-9).

Certainly no moral teacher, no prophet, however impressive, could break the bands of death or take our iniquities upon him and thus satisfy the demands of justice! Thought-leaders and founders of other world religions have made no such declarative claims of atoning divinity for themselves, though millions upon millions venerate these leaders. No wonder the Book of Mormon was urgently needed for "the convincing of the Jew and Gentile that Jesus is the Christ" (Book of Mormon title page). Passive acknowledgment of Jesus is not enough. Uninformed, however, many remain unconvinced. Hence such testifying and convincing is the purpose of all scripture, just as John stated: "But these are written, that ye might believe that Jesus is the Christ, the Son of God; and that believing ye might have life through his name" (John 20:31).

Of the Christ-centered plan of salvation, Lehi declared, "How great the importance to make these things known unto the inhabitants of the earth" (2 Nephi 2:8). Each portion of the Restoration not only affirms the reality of a redeeming Christ but also informs us that He has set the example for us as to the qualities we are to develop. Each divine disclosure deepens our regard for Him, our exemplar.

Jesus is even described as the Father, because under Elohim's direction he is the Father-Creator of this and other worlds (see D&C 76:24). Furthermore, He is the Father of all who are born again spiritually. When we take upon ourselves His name and covenant to keep His commandments, it is then that we become His sons and daughters, "the children of Christ." (See Mosiah 5:3–7; 15:1–5; 27:24–29.)

As observed by the First Presidency and Twelve in a doctrinal statement:

> Men may become children of Jesus Christ by being born anew—born of God. . . . Those who have been born unto God through obedience to the Gospel may by valiant devotion to righteousness obtain exaltation and even reach the status of godhood. . . . By the new birth—that of water and the Spirit—mankind may become children of Jesus Christ, being through the means of Him provided "begotten sons and daughters unto God" (D&C 76:24). . . .
>
> If it be proper to speak of those who accept and abide in the Gospel as Christ's sons and daughters—and upon this matter the scriptures are explicit and cannot be gainsaid or denied—it is consistently proper to speak of Jesus Christ as the Father of the righteous, they having become His children and He having been made their Father through the second birth—the baptismal regeneration. (In James E. Talmage, *The Articles of Faith* [Salt Lake City: The Church of Jesus Christ of Latter-day Saints, 1966], p. 470.)

Is it possible, regardless of their varied intensity and frequency, that the nature of the tests each of those receives who display "valiant devotion to righteousness" is essentially the same? Readily granted are the differences in degrees and "mix" as to our individual needs for particular developmental experiences. But since the desired outcomes—the cardinal qualities—are the same for all, should we be surprised at the striking similarity in the shaping clinical experiences? We too, by experiences, are to "know according to the flesh" (Alma 7:11–12). We are also to learn by our own experience. As a result of this process, things sink into the marrow of our souls; these become a portable part of us.

Looking to God, however, often involves waiting upon His timetable: "Stop, and stand still until I command thee, and I will provide means" (D&C 5:34). Waiting is difficult for children. We can accept His declarations more easily if we realize that God has told us "all things must come to pass in their time" (D&C 64:32). Further, He will hasten His work (see D&C 88:73). On the one hand we must be very careful about trying to get ahead of His timetable; yet on the other, by its very nature, superficial discipleship is impatient.

The mother of James and John sought special status for her children in the world to come: to sit on Jesus' right and left. Jesus replied, "Ye know not what ye ask" (Matthew 20:22). We can ask amiss if we are not careful (see James 4:3; 2 Nephi 4:35). We can trample revelations under foot so that they are lost in the shuffle of daily life (see 1 Nephi 19:7). We can "despise . . . the revelations of God" (Jacob 4:8). We can find ourselves persuaded by those who are not commanded of God (see D&C 30:2). But if we are seeking to be true disciples we will not ask the Lord for that which we "ought not" (D&C 8:10). We will not trifle childishly with sacred things (see D&C 6:12).

The world desperately needs divine declarations and instructions concerning what we worship, *why* we are here, and *how* we should live—certitude about what is right and wrong, conviction on what is true and what is false. Much needed, therefore, is the Restoration's verification of the reality of the resurrection. Likewise so needed is its clarification as to the nature of God and of man. Much needed as well is the Restoration's enunciation of the divinely determined purposes of this mortal existence.

Those who have lived in the midst of the famine foreseen by Amos, one of not hearing the full word of God (Amos 8:11–12), have never known the taste and nourishment of the whole-grain gospel. Instead, some have subsisted on the fast foods of philosophy. When Jesus described himself as the nourishing Bread of Life, it caused some to walk no more with Him (see John 6:66). No wonder Jesus was moved to say, "Blessed is he, whosoever shall not be offended in me" (Matthew 11:6; see also John 6:61). To which it might be added, "Blessed is he who is not offended by the Restoration"!

Too little attention is paid to the remarkable refreshment, both spiritual and intellectual, brought by the Restoration. First, God the Father really lives. Next, Jesus, God's beloved first-born Son and the Only Begotten in the flesh, lives and has been resurrected. Next, fresh scriptures not only testify that Jesus is the Christ but also that life has meaning and purpose, and that all mankind will be resurrected. Further, besides the Savior Himself many other resurrected beings have ministered, giving instructions and ordinations and conferring priesthood keys, all needed to help in the perfecting of the Saints. There were many angels at the dedication of the Kirtland Temple on March 27, 1836. The Prophet elsewhere refers to "divers angels, from Michael or Adam down to the present time" (D&C 128:20–21). Those heavenly visitors were not mute. Joseph was ordained by them, received keys from them, and was instructed and directed by them.

The Restoration is really just beginning its spreading influence among the human family. This freshening is occurring at a time when, for many humans at least, the long interval without divine manifestations and revelations has created doubt and uncertainty. The freshening has come at a time when the weight of the world's cares is too much with us. For many, alas, there has been too much elapsed time, causing relapsed religion. True, even though the earthly interval during which individuals are to walk by faith is never very long, the seemingly long period of cumulative and collective time is used against God by disbelievers and the indifferent.

In any case, the world is marching ever more determinedly to its own cadence, dealing religion out as being irrelevant.

Not many welcome the Restoration: it interferes with the seemingly uninterrupted flow of secular things, symbolized by the repetitive "eating, drinking, and giving in marriage," or the routine focus of life. Peter foresaw that scoffers in the last days would say: "Where is the promise of his coming? for since the fathers fell asleep, all things continue as they were from the beginning of the creation." Peter observed further that the Lord's long-suffering would even be used against Him, since the scoffers were "willingly ignorant." He then reminded members of the Church, "What manner of [persons] ought ye to be" as differentiated from those "of the world." (2 Peter 3:4, 5, 11.)

The coming of the Restoration with its inspiring and initiating First Vision set in motion the possibility of correcting the enormous error which besets so much of mankind. The Restoration brought correct views about the nature of man, about the nature of God, and about the nature of man's relationship to God. Yet as the Prophet Joseph observed, very few mortals will try to understand, having little interest in comprehending "that which is past" (Joseph Fielding Smith, comp., *Teachings of the Prophet Joseph Smith* [Salt Lake City: Deseret Book Company, 1976], p. 343). Laman and Lemuel did not understand the dealings of the God who had created them (1 Nephi 2:12). It was prophesied that in the last days other skeptics would be "willingly ignorant" regarding the doings of people who lived in another time and place (see 2 Peter 3:5). Just the opposite, the Restoration promises that one day we will have the scriptures of the lost tribes of Israel, and we will understand further God's dealings with another people in another time and place (see 2 Nephi 29:13).

Where people fail to comprehend the redemptive designs of God they fall into an enormous error. The pattern of living which then emerges is one in which people tend to get on with the routine of life, which carries its own concerns. Thus the protracted period of human history without prophets is seen by many mortals as a negation of God, or at least as an indication of a God uninvolved with people on this planet.

How vital, therefore, for us to know the realities: There is a plan of salvation; there was an apostasy; and now there has been a restoration. God has given man moral agency, leaving him free to believe or disbelieve, or to disregard the divine and spiritual evidence. Thus an incredible irony emerges: As people become less believing there are fewer spiritual experiences, and this is twisted by the disbeliever into confirmation of his premises.

Mortality is divinely designed so that we are to walk by faith, but even this is used against God. As people come to have less and less faith, some are more demanding of absolute proof if they are going to believe at all.

The Restoration was not just a single instance of God's having been seen by man; rather, it features a series of remarkable episodes with striking interior consistency. This relieves the routineness of the mortal scene—at least for those who have eyes to see and ears to hear. Otherwise, doubt and despair result in a view that "man is alone," with variations of the view "eat, drink, and be merry . . . , for tomorrow we die" (2 Nephi 28:8) and the assumption that when a man is dead "that [is] the end thereof" (Alma 30:18). If, therefore, man is alone, why not please himself, and as much as he likes? How different a course from that pursued by those striving to become the men and women of Christ!

The pages of Restoration scriptures ripple and resound with innumerable essential truths. For example, through re-

vealed Christology we learn about Christ's premortal pin-
nacle as a Creator-God; and that, despite this preeminence,
only later did He receive a fulness (see D&C 93:12–13, 16).

The Lord has told us how important it is to understand
not only "what" we worship but also "how" to worship (see
D&C 93:19; see also John 4:22). Real adoration of the Father
and Jesus results in the emulation of them! How shall we
know how to become more like them if we do not know
about their character and nature? Inquired King Benjamin of
the consequences of estrangement, "How knoweth a man the
master whom he has not served, and who is a stranger unto
him, and is far from the thoughts and intents of his heart?"
(Mosiah 5:13.)

The Restoration also helps us understand how the school-
master law of Moses was a preparing and foretelling type,
without which we will not understand dispensationalism, including the particular place of meridian Christianity in the
stream of religious history.

> It is expedient that ye should keep the law of Moses as yet;
> but I say unto you, that the time shall come when it shall
> no more be expedient. . . .
>   . . . [For] God himself should come down among the
> children of men, and take upon him the form of man, and
> go forth in mighty power upon the face of the earth.
> (Mosiah 13:27, 34; see also 13:29–35; 16:14; 3:15; Galatians
> 3:24.)

For moderns, the relevancy of the Restoration message is
special. For instance, we are clearly indebted to our British
ancestors for our precious King James Bible. Yet that nation
subsequently suffered from a wave of irreligion. Academic
Vice-President Stan L. Albrecht of Brigham Young University wrote of that wave of irreligion:

> In the middle 1850s [there began a] pattern of downturn in
> religious activity in British society. . . . "Agnosticism [was
> made] respectable if not universal by the turn of the cen-

tury." . . . By the early 1900s Arnold Bennett could say, ". . . The intelligentsia has sat back, shrugged its shoulders, given a sigh of relief, and decreed tacitly or by plain statement: 'The affair is over and done with.' "

. . . By the 1970s only about 5 percent of the adult population in the Church of England even attended Easter religious services, and the percentage continues to decline. (Stan L. Albrecht, "The Consequential Dimension of Mormon Religiosity," *BYU Studies*, Spring 1989, p. 98.)

Yet if we read the scriptures repetitively they will inform and inspire us; they will enthrall us, again and again. Neglected scriptures mean agnostic citizens. Ordinary books contain comparative crumbs, whereas the Bread of Life provides us with an endless feast.

We learn from the scriptures that salvation is specific, not vague; it includes individual resurrection and triumph over death. We will stand before God, as individuals, and kneel and confess (see Alma 12:13–15, 34–35). The faithful will even sit down, as individuals, with the spiritual notables of ages past, for God has said He will "land their souls, yea, their immortal souls, at the right hand of God in the kingdom of heaven, to sit down with Abraham, and Isaac, and with Jacob, and with all our holy fathers, to go no more out" (Helaman 3:30; see also Alma 7:25; Matthew 8:11; D&C 124:19).

We will not be merged into some unremembering molecular mass. Nor will we be mere droplets in an ocean of consciousness. In one way or another, sooner or later, all individuals will plead, as Alma did at his turning point, "O Jesus, thou Son of God, have mercy on me" (Alma 36:18).

Thus as Latter-day Saints and children of Christ we have enlarged perspectives, because "through the infinite goodness of God, and the manifestations of his Spirit, [we] have great views of that which is to come" (Mosiah 5:3).

In contrast many today, like some among the Book of Mormon peoples, believe that "when a man [is] dead, that [is] the end thereof" (Alma 30:18). For such, there are certain existential "givens." Two examples are: "There is no built-in scheme of meaning in the world" (Irvin D. Yalom, Stanford University psychiatrist, "Exploring Psychic Interiors," *U.S. News & World Report,* October 30, 1989, p. 67). "No deity will save us; we must save ourselves" ("Humanist Manifesto II," "Liberal Family," *The Encyclopedia of American Religions: Religious Creeds,* J. Gordon Melton, ed. [Detroit: Gale Research Company, 1988], p. 641).

No wonder the Restoration is so relevant and so urgent, having been given so "that faith also might increase in the earth" (D&C 1:21).

Compared to the great, divine declarations which are central to real faith, what else matters? To illustrate, two Book of Mormon prophets in referring to a lesser concern, death, used the phrases "it mattereth not" or "it matters not" (Ether 15:34; Mosiah 13:9).

Fortunately for mankind, the reality of the Atonement does not depend upon either our awareness of it or our acceptance of it! Immortality is a free gift to all, including the presently unappreciative and unbelieving (2 Nephi 2:4).

Meanwhile, even those who are spiritually sensitive feel less than full joy in this life because "our lifelong nostalgia, our longing to be reunited with something in the universe from which we now feel cut off, to be on the inside of some door which we have always seen from the outside, is . . . the truest index of our real situation" (C. S. Lewis, *A Mind Awake* [New York: Harcourt, Brace & World, Inc., 1968], p. 23).

In that sense we are all prodigals! We, too, must come to ourselves, having determined "I will arise and go to my father" (Luke 15:18). This reunion and reconciliation is actually possible. Because of the Atonement, we are not irrevocably cut off.

The "children of Christ," the "children of light," in any dispensation willingly make the sacrifice of a broken heart and a contrite spirit (see 3 Nephi 9:20; D&C 59:8; Psalm 51:17; Ephesians 5:8). The children of Christ are meek and malleable—their hearts can be broken, changed, or made anew. The child of Christ can eventually mature spiritually to become the "new" man or woman, the man or woman of Christ.

But first we must become men and women "in understanding" (1 Corinthians 14:20).

CHAPTER 4

"The Man of Christ"

The virtues of the children of Christ who become the men and women of Christ are cardinal, portable, and eternal. They reflect the outcome of serious discipleship. For instance, true disciples will continue to grow spiritually, because they have "faith unto repentance," giving them the vital capacity to improve (see Alma 34:16, 17; 13:10). To the degree developed, these cardinal qualities will finally rise with us in the resurrection and will give us "so much the advantage in the world to come" (D&C 130:19). Their development represents that "[laying] hold upon the word of God" that can "lead the man [and woman] of Christ" to a place "at the right hand of God in the kingdom of heaven" (Helaman 3:29–30).

As we contemplate the qualities in this cluster, each reminds us of the need to tame our egos. Blessed is the person who is progressing in the taming of his or her egoistic self.

King Benjamin, for example, had not the least desire to boast of himself (see Mosiah 2:16). He was unconcerned with projecting his political image, because he had Christ's image in his countenance. We are instructed not only in what we are to become, but also in what we are to avoid. Abinadi noted that Jesus suffered temptation but yielded not (Mosiah 15:5). Unlike many of us, Christ gave no heed to temptations (D&C 20:22). This is yet another instructive example to His children, for, even when we later evict temptations, we so often have entertained them first.

The development of the cardinal virtues is central to God's plans for each of us. Lack of this perspective about His plans for us is part of the failure of Laman and Lemuel: "And thus Laman and Lemuel, . . . did murmur because they knew not the dealings of that God who had created them" (1 Nephi 2:12; see also Mosiah 10:14). Though the brass plates were in their possession, they missed the significance of "the doings of the Lord in other lands, among people of old" (1 Nephi 19:22).

How "plain and precious," therefore, are the holy scriptures, which tell us of the dealings and doings of the Lord over the sweep of history! Are not all of us in need of such perspective?

The men and women of Christ understand the importance of feasting regularly on sacred records that testify of Jesus (see 2 Nephi 31:20; 32:3; Jacob 2:9; Joseph Smith— Matthew 1:37). Without such records, belief in Him and in the glorious resurrection can quickly wane:

> And at the time that Mosiah discovered them, . . . their language had become corrupted; and they had brought no records with them; and they denied the being of their Creator (Omni 1:17).

> There were many of the rising generation that could not understand the words of king Benjamin, being little children at the time he spake unto his people; and they did not believe the tradition of their fathers.

They did not believe what had been said concerning the resurrection of the dead, neither did they believe concerning the coming of Christ. (Mosiah 26:1-2.)

Parents who are either untaught or unheeding of the essential gospel truths will probably witness the lapse of real faith in Christ in their children.

As we accept Christ and become His children, a change begins in us—even a "mighty change." As we earnestly strive to become one with Him, being swallowed up in His purposes, we come to resemble Him. Christ who has saved us thus becomes the father of our salvation, and we have His image increasingly in our countenances and conduct. (See Mosiah 5:7.)

Since His qualities are to be emulated by His children, as the Prophet Joseph Smith taught us, it is vital for us to comprehend the character and personality of God (see Joseph Fielding Smith, comp., *Teachings of the Prophet Joseph Smith* [Salt Lake City: Deseret Book Company, 1976], p. 343). Hence the value of the scriptures, if we are really to comprehend ourselves.

As we strive in our growing maturity to truly emulate Jesus' example we will thereby encounter the costs of discipleship. Through our own micro-experiences we will come to know what it is to suffer and to be reproached for taking upon ourselves the name of Christ (see Luke 6:22; 1 Peter 4:14). Therefore, our fiery trials, said Peter, should not be thought of as "some strange thing" (1 Peter 4:12). As we are believing and trusting we become more Christ-like; and this becomes more evident in our daily lives, whether in the treatment of the poor (see Mosiah 4:16) or in our share of the management of civic affairs. Ammon taught, for instance, of how those who so change will truly be "of great benefit to [their] fellow beings" (Mosiah 8:18). Alma learned from the Lord that the enlightened individual can actually evoke faith in other people by "his words alone" (Mosiah 26:15-16; see also 3 Nephi 11:2; D&C 46:13-14).

King Benjamin said, "I would that ye should . . . always retain in remembrance, the greatness of God, and your own nothingness, and his goodness and long-suffering towards you" (Mosiah 4:11; see also Moses 1:9–10). We who have the Restoration scriptures have further reasons to feel over-whelmed by the greatness of God. Those scriptures tell us that there is no space in which there is no kingdom (see D&C 88:37). God's works are without end, and He has created worlds which are "innumerable unto man" (see Moses 1:4, 33, 35). The very heavens and planets witness that there is a Supreme Creator (Alma 30:44). On Judgment Day, declared the repentant Alma, everyone at that assemblage will "confess that [God] is God" (Mosiah 27:31). What could be more basic for mortals who have walked after the image of their own god? (See D&C 1:16.)

When one considers history's disbelieving notables who will be there, these next lines are especially subduing: "Then shall they confess, who live without God in the world, that the judgment of an everlasting punishment is just upon them; and they shall quake, and tremble, and shrink beneath the glance of his all-searching eye" (Mosiah 27:31; see also Mosiah 16:1; Alma 12:15).

The faithful, however, are in a much happier situation. They "shall stand before him" and "see his face with plea-sure" (Enos 1:27). His all-searching eyes will likewise ema-nate perfect, overwhelming love, a love which, alas, too few will have reciprocated. The sense of undeservingness will be deep and profound!

Meanwhile, if during this life we are without enlighten-ment as to the plan of salvation we will continue to experi-ence the unwelcome sense "of having ended a chapter. One more portion of one's self slipping away into the past." (C. S. Lewis, *Letters of C. S. Lewis* [London: Geoffrey Bles, Ltd., 1966], p. 306.)

In her study *Memory*, Mary Warnock wrote: "Anything that is *over*. . . . is a lost *possession*. . . . The past is a para-dise from which we are necessarily excluded." (As quoted in

Dan Jacobson, "Of Time and Poetry," *Commentary*, November 1989, p. 52.)

Thomas Hardy's memories, Dan Jacobson wrote, "speak constantly to him of experiences once shared that are now his alone. . . . The past continually comes to him; but he knows that he can never go back to it." ("Of Time and Poetry," p. 52.)

But one day it will come back fully and resplendently for those who are to be eternally enlightened!

But even now as Latter-day Saints we know whose we are, whence we came, why we are here, and what manner of men and women we are meant to become (see 2 Peter 3:11; 3 Nephi 27:27). Still, like Alma, we will "long to be there" (Alma 36:22), in the "royal courts on high." It is the only destination that really matters. Resplendent reunion awaits us! What is more reasonable and more wonderful than children going home? Especially to a home where the past, the present, and the future form an everlasting and eternal now! (See D&C 130:7; 38:2; Smith, *Teachings*, p. 220.)

Therefore, let us "believe in God; believe that he is, and that he created all things, both in heaven and in earth; believe that he has all wisdom, and all power, both in heaven and in earth; believe that man doth not comprehend all the things which the Lord can comprehend" (Mosiah 4:9).

In this life, meanwhile, how can there be refining fires without heat? Or greater patience without some instructive waiting? Or more empathy without first bearing one another's burdens? Not only that their burdens may be lightened, but that we may thereby be enlightened by greater empathy. Or how can there be increased individual faith without some customized uncertainty? Or learning to live in cheerful insecurity without some insecurity? How can there be later magnification without some present deprivation?

Except we are thus tutored, how else shall we grow spiritually to become men and women of Christ? In this brief span of mortality, therefore, with so much to learn, reveries are often quickly, even rudely, elbowed aside by tutoring adversities. As faithful children, we are to learn to be "willing to submit" to our perfect Father (Mosiah 3:19).

At times we may feel overwhelmed by our callings and circumstances. Then we genuinely need vital perspective and reassurance about what matters most — which is keeping our covenants.

At other times we may feel underwhelmed and underused in terms of our formal Church callings or civic chores, but we can never honestly feel underwhelmed in terms of the call we all have from Jesus to become, virtue by virtue, as He is (see 3 Nephi 27:27). For the moment, official duties and official roles may seem, for some, insufficient. But as a neighbor no one of us will ever fully use the abundant opportunities for service which lie all about us.

There are clear and basic scriptures describing the spiritual substance and qualities that men and women of Christ are to strive to achieve in their lives. When significantly developed, these qualities convey the added authority of example. Thus, rather than be intimidated by the general concept of "perfection," if we will strive specifically to become more loving, more patient, and so forth, genuine progress is possible.

These qualities are *cardinal* and *eternal*. They are *portable* and at death will go with us through the veil. Jesus Himself set the standard: "What manner of men ought ye to be? Verily I say unto you, even as I am." (3 Nephi 27:27.)

King Benjamin defined the saintliness to be achieved. The disciple was to

[become] a saint . . . *submissive, meek, humble, patient, full of love, willing to submit* to all things which the Lord seeth fit to inflict upon him, even as a child doth submit to his father (Mosiah 3:19, italics added).

After all, Latter-day Saints should have a special interest in what is required to become a Saint. Here are other directive scriptures that confirm the necessity of certain key qualities and add a few others.

And now I would that ye should be humble, and be submissive and *gentle; easy to be entreated;* full of patience and
long-suffering; being *temperate* in all things (Alma 7:23,
italics added).

Be led by the Holy Spirit, becoming humble, meek, submissive, patient, full of love and all *long-suffering* (Alma 13:28,
italics added).

Our spiritual substance will be reflected in our worship
and our life-style. We are to work

by persuasion, by long-suffering, by gentleness and meekness, and by *love unfeigned;* by *kindness* (D&C 121:41–42,
italics added).

The same central attributes are necessary in order for us
to qualify for the ministry.

And faith, hope, charity and love, with an eye single to
the glory of God, qualify him for the work.
Remember faith, virtue, knowledge, temperance, patience, brotherly kindness, godliness, charity, humility, diligence. (D&C 4:6–7.)

The Lord advises us that "no one can assist in this work
except he shall be humble and full of love, having faith,
hope, charity, being temperate in all things" (D&C 12:8).
Thus we see not only the centrality but also the needed con-
stancy of these qualities. This is true of all levels of service in
God's kingdom; for instance, He has instructed that the decisions of the First Presidency, the Quorum of the Twelve,
and the Quorums of Seventy are to be made in ways that reflect these same cardinal virtues: "The decisions of these
quorums, or either of them, are to be made in all righteousness, in holiness, and lowliness of heart, meekness and long
suffering, and in faith, and virtue, and knowledge, temperance, patience, godliness, brotherly kindness and charity"
(D&C 107:30).

In a Church and world full of imperfect people we are wise to make allowances for individual differences and also for the shaping variations in our individual experiences and gifts. We surely do come in different packages! Even so, the present "package" which constitutes oneself should not be the ultimate package or self.

Too often when we seek to excuse ourselves it is ironical that we are excusing "the natural man." Yet scriptures inform us that the natural man is to be *put off;* he is too heavy and too fatiguing to carry (see Mosiah 3:19). He should not be *kept on* because of a mistaken and self-demeaning sense that the natural man constitutes our individuality.

There are a few matters of mere preference which involve no moral content, such as one's favorite color. But we must take care not to expand the legitimate zone of personal preference naively and carelessly. It is one thing to have little interest in developing a garden and quite another to have little interest in developing people—especially developing oneself in the cardinal virtues.

Perhaps of a few things we can properly say, "That's how I am!" But of the many things—all those involving spiritual consequences, some obvious, some subtle—we cannot justifiably say, "That's how I am!" Instead, we have a solemn obligation to strive to become like Jesus by putting off the natural package, and this also helps by lightening our load for the journey along the straight and narrow path.

It is one thing to say we have little interest in sports and quite another to say that we have little interest in becoming more patient in our relationships with others. How can we become as the Savior is if we remain impatient?

We may enjoy listening to a symphony but disdain listening to children. Yet can we conceive of praying to a non-listening God?

What is being urged on these pages is not frantic self-concern, immobilizing guilt, or destructive self-criticism; rather, it is simply coming to terms, over time and wisely, with the differences between what we are and what we should be and have the power to become. We must be wise and tolerant, making allowances for the frailties and differences in each other. Nor should we be too harsh in judging ourselves, either; instead, we need to continue in patience in spite of recognizing our faults.

Thus serious discipleship neither expects perfection in others nor denies the need to progress toward it in oneself.

One person might have abilities demonstrably greater than those of his peers, yet this would be no excuse to avoid the wise delegation of significant tasks to them. After all, a perfect God shares His work with us.

There are too many scriptural examples of pointed tutoring for us to ignore them. One might have commendable loyalty for others, but this is no reason to forego giving them needed developmental counsel while speaking "the truth in love" (Ephesians 4:15). Jethro surely did his duty with Moses, to whom he doubtless was loyal and nurturing (see Exodus 18:13–23).

Oliver Cowdery, eager to translate, was told after he failed that it was because he was intellectually lazy and did not continue as he commenced (see D&C 9:5, 7). The righteous young man who had kept the commandments from his youth up was told deliberately by Jesus, "One thing thou lackest." We read of the inquiring young man that "Jesus beholding him loved him"—loved him enough to tutor him. (See Mark 10:21.)

Jesus, our perfect model, had His own perfect model:

> Then answered Jesus and said unto them, Verily, verily, I say unto you, The Son can do nothing of himself, but what he seeth the Father do: for what things soever he doeth, these also doeth the Son likewise (John 5:19).

Just what was seen and emulated by Jesus (in both first and second estates) we do not know, but the point is clear.

The following exemplifications and admonitions as to attributes make it clear that these are not optional if we would follow Him:

Ye shall be holy; for I am holy (Leviticus 11:44).

And the Lord passed by before him, and proclaimed, the Lord, the Lord God, merciful and gracious, longsuffering, and abundant in goodness and truth (Exodus 34:6).

I say unto you, if ye have come to a knowledge of the goodness of God, and his matchless power, and his wisdom, and his patience, and his long-suffering towards the children of men . . . (Mosiah 4:6).

Be ye therefore merciful, as your Father also is merciful (Luke 6:36).

For I have given you an example, that ye should do as I have done to you (John 13:15).

Jesus Christ [shows] forth all long-suffering, for a pattern to them which should hereafter believe on him to life everlasting (1 Timothy 1:16).

Christ also suffered for us, leaving us an example, that ye should follow his steps (1 Peter 2:21).

And again, it showeth unto the children of men the straitness of the path, and the narrowness of the gate, by which they should enter, he having set the example before them (2 Nephi 31:9).

Be ye therefore perfect, even as your Father which is in heaven is perfect (Matthew 5:48).

After His perfection, Jesus included Himself as our model:

Therefore I would that ye should be perfect even as I, or your Father who is in heaven is perfect (3 Nephi 12:48).

Therefore, what manner of men ought ye to be? Verily I say unto you, even as I am. (3 Nephi 27:27.)

Ye know the things that ye must do in my church; for the works which ye have seen me do that shall ye also do; for that which ye have seen me do even that shall ye do (3 Nephi 27:21).

Behold I am the light; I have set an example for you (3 Nephi 18:16).

The Prophet Joseph Smith taught:

If you wish to go where God is, you must be like God, or possess the principles which God possesses (Smith, Teachings, p. 216).

While we should be understanding of imperfections, we should also understand how, with our responsiveness to God's tutoring, weak things can actually enable us to "become strong," and why childish things must be "put away" (Ether 12:26-27; 1 Corinthians 13:11).

We all need encouragement, but we need it without indulgence. Moses did not say to Jethro, "Look, I work diligently. This is how I am!" By the way, Moses quickly took the counsel to delegate, doubtless because, scriptures inform us, he was the most meek man "upon the face of the earth" (Numbers 12:3).

From what we have discussed, it follows that "working out our salvation" and exaltation includes keeping the commandments, but it also includes working out the development of these virtues in our lives.

Given the tremendous importance of these cardinal virtues, both in this world and in the world to come, should we be surprised if, to hasten the process, the Lord regularly, if not daily, gives us the relevant and necessary clinical experiences? In this way the impatient will be given chances to become more patient, the unmerciful to become more merciful.

By serving Jesus and by thinking of Him we draw closer to Him and are enlightened. Otherwise, we become estranged from His exemplification as well as from Him (see Mosiah 5:13).

In summation, these cardinal virtues are intertwined, interactive, and interdependent:

We Are to Be:	*We Are Not to Be:*
1. Meek and humble	Self-concerned, dismissive, proud, seeking ascendancy, needlessly making others anxious and insecure
2. Patient	Hectic, hurried, pushy, manipulative, unhelpfully intolerant of ineptness
3. Full of love	Demanding, dominating, harsh, manipulative, condescending
4. Gentle	Coarse, brusque, vindictive
5. Easily entreated	Unapproachable, rejecting, inaccessible, non-listening, and stereotyping of others
6. Long-suffering	Impatient, disinterested, curt, easily offended

7. Submissive to God	Resistant to the Spirit, life's lessons, and instructive feedback, and unwilling to endure
8. Temperate (Self-restrained)	Egoistic, eager for attention and recognition, and too talkative
9. Merciful	Judgmental and unforgiving
10. Gracious	Tactless, easily irritated, ungenerous
11. Holy	Worldly

He who is most meek and lowly has instructed us, "Take my yoke upon you, and learn of me; for I am meek and lowly in heart" (Matthew 11:29). Accepting that yoke means that we too need to be meek and lowly.

Lest we worry overmuch that our meekness might be an open invitation for others to abuse us, it is well to note some of its less-understood features. For example, meekness may not always "win," especially in worldly matters or in the short run; but in the long run the meek will inherit the earth. And meekness is not the acceptance of imposition; it can still be firm, still insist on fairness, even reprove with sharpness on occasion. Meekness also can ask inspired, piercing questions. Meekness impels us to speak the truth in love. Meekness brings its own compensatory blessings, especially that of an enhanced direction from the Holy Spirit.

Nor is meekness without its mortal models who have succeeded even in the world's views. A prominent example is George Washington, of whom it has been written: "In all history few men who possessed unassailable power have used that power so gently and self-effacingly for what their best instincts told them was the welfare of their neighbors and all mankind" (James Thomas Flexner, *Washington: The Indispensable Man* [New York: Plume, 1984], p. xvi).

As to scriptural examples, "The man Moses was very meek, above all the men which were upon the face of the earth" (Numbers 12:3). And the great prophet John the Baptist, who could blisteringly denounce as vipers the hypocritical leaders who appeared at his Jordan River baptisms (see Matthew 3:7), meekly defended Jesus and His proselyting success with the self-effacing words, "He must increase, but I must decrease" (John 3:30).

The ultimate model of meekness is Jesus, the most effective and the most intelligent person who has ever lived. It is no coincidence that He also was the most meek. Meekness, then, is a saintly quality, and therefore of Deity. When we take his yoke upon us, in our small ways we can best learn of Jesus and of His meekness and lowliness. Then, as divine attributes are painfully and slowly developed in us, we marvel the more at His having perfected these attributes. Appreciation of Him yields to adoration and emulation of Him!

His gospel—whether truths about the nature of God, or of man, or of the universe—as taught in holy scriptures and holy temples is remarkable. The gospel is stunning as to its interior consistency, and it is breathtaking as to its exterior expansiveness. Rather than being without the gospel and thus in a mortal maze, "I stand all amazed!" (*Hymns,* no. 193.) The spiritual facts that emerge soon encompass and testify about "the goodness of God, and his matchless power, and his wisdom, and his patience, and his long-suffering towards the children of men" (Mosiah 4:6).

For us to know such transcending things helps us to endure the journey and the ironies of life as we mature into men and women of Christ who can endure well and hold fast —even when there are injections of irony.

CHAPTER 5

"Endure it Well. . . . Valiantly"

The following wintry verse instructs and reminds us of one of the most central and regular challenges for the men and women of Christ:

> Nevertheless the Lord seeth fit to chasten his people; yea, he trieth their patience and their faith (Mosiah 23:21).

Such declarations of divine purpose ought to keep us on spiritual alert as to life's purposeful adversities, especially as we seek to become more saintly. Disciples will escape neither adversity nor the irony forming the hard crust on the bread of adversity.

Irony tries both our faith and our patience. Irony can be a particularly bitter form of chastening because it involves disturbing incongruity; it involves outcomes in violation of our expectations, including what we feel we "deserved."

Sometimes it lays waste our good-intentioned and best-laid plans.

On occasion we even set up our own ironies by being too declarative and too certain. Such was the case with Peter, who said he would never deny Jesus. Peter was quickly reminded by the Savior that soon, before the rooster crowed, Peter would deny Him three times. (See Matthew 26:31–35.) In like manner today our rigidities and deficiencies sometimes may actually invite tutoring.

Perhaps a person is visibly and patiently prepared for an important role amid widespread expectation of his impending promotion. What follows, however, ends up lasting only a very narrow moment in time. A political victory may seem so near; then it recedes, and finally vanishes altogether. Without meekness such ironical circumstances are very difficult to manage.

In a marriage a careless, ego-filled declaration hardens into a rigid, well-defended position that then becomes more important than communication or reconciliation. An intellectual stand is proudly and stubbornly defended even in the face of tutoring truth or correcting counsel. Even when a position clearly proves indefensible, pride stays resolutely and stupidly at its post. This is unfortunate, because occasionally, as we all know, humbly backing off is really going forward.

With its inverting of the anticipated consequences, irony becomes the frequent cause of an individual's being offended. The larger and the more untamed a person's ego, the greater the likelihood of his being offended, especially when tasting his portion of vinegar and gall. Words may issue: "Why me?" "Why this?" "Why now?" It is hoped such words will give way to subsequent spiritual composure; but when such words precede bitter inconsolability, then it is a surprisingly short distance to bitterness. Amid life's varied ironies we may begin to wonder: "Didn't God notice this torturous turn of events? And if He noticed, why did He permit it? Am I not valued? Didn't I deserve better?"

Our planning usually assumes that our destiny is largely in our own hands. Then come intruding events, first elbowing aside, then evicting, what we had anticipated and even earned. Hence we can be offended by events as well as by people.

Irony may involve not only unexpected suffering but also undeserved suffering. We feel we deserved better, and yet we fared worse. We had other plans—even commendable plans; did they not count? For example, a physician who trained laboriously to help the sick cannot do so now because of his own illness. For a period, because of constraining circumstances, a diligent prophet of the Lord was an "idle witness" (Mormon 3:16). Frustrating conditions keep more than a few of us from making our appointed rounds. Customized challenges are thus added to that affliction and temptation that Paul described as "common to man" (1 Corinthians 10:13).

In coping with irony, as in all things, we have an exemplary teacher in Jesus, whose divinity was assaulted almost constantly. For Jesus, irony began at His birth. Truly, He "suffered the will of the Father in all things from the beginning" (3 Nephi 11:11). This whole earth was Jesus' footstool (see Acts 7:49); He created it; yet at Bethlehem there was "no room . . . in the inn" (Luke 2:7) and "no crib for his bed" (Hymns, no. 206).

At the end, meek and lowly Jesus partook of the most bitter cup without becoming the least bitter (see 3 Nephi 11:11; D&C 19:18–19). The most innocent one suffered the most. Yet the King of kings did not break, even when some of His subjects did to Him "as they listed" (D&C 49:6). Christ's unyielding capacity to endure such irony was truly remarkable. You and I are so much more brittle. For instance, we forget that, by their very nature, many tests are unfair.

In heaven, Christ's lofty name was determined to be the only name on earth offering salvation to all mankind (see Acts 4:12; 2 Nephi 25:20; see also Abraham 3:27), yet the

King of kings, the Mortal Messiah, willingly lived modestly, wrote Paul, even as a person "of no reputation" (Philippians 2:7).

What a contrast to our maneuvering over relative recognition and comparative status! How different, too, from the ways in which some among us mistakenly see the size and response of their audiences as the sole verification of their worth! Yet those fickle galleries to which we sometimes play have a way of being rotated and emptied. They will surely be empty on Judgment Day; everyone will be somewhere else — on their knees.

As the Creator, Christ constructed the universe; yet in little Galilee He was known merely as "the carpenter's son" (Matthew 13:55). In fact, the Lord of the universe was without honor even in His own Nazarene countryside. Though astonished at His teachings, his neighbors "were offended at him." Even meek Jesus "marvelled because of their unbelief." (Mark 6:3, 6.)

As Jehovah, Jesus issued the original commandment to keep the Sabbath day holy, but during His mortal messiahship He was accused of violating the Sabbath because on that day He gave healing rest to the afflicted (see John 5:8–16). Can we absorb the irony of being hurt while trying to help? When, having done good, we are misrepresented, can we watch the feathers of false witness scatter on the winds without our becoming rattled or resentful?

Long, long ago as Creator, Christ provided habitable conditions for us on this earth, generously providing all the essential atmospheric conditions for life, including essential water (see Moses 1:33; D&C 76:24). Yet on the cross, when He was aflame with thirst, "they gave him vinegar to drink mingled with gall: and when he had tasted thereof, he would not drink" (Matthew 27:34; see also Psalm 69:21). Even so, Jesus was not a railing man but a forgiving Christ (see Luke 23:34).

Christ was keenly aware of the constant irony: "Foxes have holes, and birds of the air have nests; but the Son of man hath not where to lay his head" (Luke 9:58). He asked a treacherous Judas, "Betrayest thou the Son of man with a kiss?" (Luke 22:48.) And earlier he uttered the soulful lament: "O, Jerusalem, Jerusalem, . . . how often would I have gathered thy children together, even as a hen gathereth her chickens under her wings, and ye would not!" (Matthew 23:37.) The ritual of rejection was happening to Jesus all over again.

We all know what it is like not to be listened to, but, worse, how about disdain or even contempt? Whatever its decibel level, however, there is a difference between noticing rejection, as Jesus did, and railing against rejection, as He did not.

As the Creator, Christ fashioned "worlds without number" (Moses 1:33), yet with His fingers He fashioned a little clay from dirt and spittle, restoring sight to one blind man (see John 9:6). Thus the greatest meekly ministered "unto one of the least of these" (Matthew 25:40). Do you and I understand that the significance of our service does not depend upon its scale?

Within a few hours Christ would rescue all mankind, yet he heard the manipulated crowd cry, "Barabbas," thereby rescuing a life-taking murderer instead of life-giving Jesus (see Mark 15:7-15).

Can we remain true amid false justice? Will we do our duty against the will of the roar of the crowd? In the Master Teacher's tailoring of His tutoring, depending upon the spiritual readiness of His pupils, we see instructive irony even in some of these episodes.

To the healed leper returning with gratitude, Jesus' searching but simple query was, "Where are the [other] nine?" (Luke 17:17.) To a more knowledgeable mother of Apostles, desiring that her two sons sit on Jesus' right and left hands, Jesus reprovingly but lovingly said, "Ye know not what you ask. . . . [This] is not mine to give." (Matthew 20:22-23.) To a grieving but rapidly maturing Peter, still burning with the memory of a rooster's crowing, thrice came the directive, "Feed my sheep," but also a statement signifying "by what death" the great Apostle would later be martyred (John 18:25–27; 21:15–19). How much more demanding of Peter than of the leper!

When a sudden, stabbing light exposes the gap between what we are and what we think we are, can we, like Peter, let that light be a healing laser? Do we have the patience to endure when one of our comparative strengths is called into question? A scalding crisis may actually be the means of stripping corrosive pride from a virtue.

To the humbly devout woman of Samaria who expected the Messiah, Jesus quietly disclosed, "I that speak unto thee am he" (John 4:26). Yet an anxious Pilate "saith unto Jesus, Whence art thou? But Jesus gave him no answer." (John 19:9.)

Can we remain silent when silence is eloquence—but may be used against us? Or will we murmur, just to let God know we notice the ironies?

Even with all the negative ironies there is the glad irony of Christ's great mission. He Himself noted that, precisely because He was "lifted up upon" the cross, He was about to "draw all men unto [him]," and after He had been "lifted up by men even so should men be lifted up by the Father" (3 Nephi 27:14).

But how can we fortify ourselves against the irony in our lives and cope better when it comes? By being more like Jesus, such as by loving more. Loving increases our absorptive capacity.

> And the world, because of their iniquity, shall judge him to be a thing of naught; wherefore they scourge him, and he suffereth it; and they smite him, and he suffereth it. Yea, they spit upon him, and he suffereth it, [Why?] because of his loving kindness and his long-suffering towards the children of men. (1 Nephi 19:9.)

There are other significant keys for coping daily with irony. "And he said to them all, If any man will come after me, let him deny himself, and take up his cross daily, and follow me" (Luke 9:23). Wise self-denial shrinks our swollen sense of entitlement.

Another cardinal key is to "live in thanksgiving daily, for the many mercies and blessings which [God] doth bestow upon you" (Alma 34:38).

Life's ironies, serious as they may seem to us, are much more than offset by heaven's many tender mercies. We cannot count all our blessings every day, but we can at least carry over the reassuring bottom line from the last counting.

Jesus exemplified another vital way of coping. Though He suffered all manner of temptations (see Alma 7:11), He "gave no heed unto them" (D&C 20:22). Unlike some of us, He did not fantasize, reconsider, or replay temptations. How is it that you and I do not seem to understand that while initially we are stronger and the temptations weaker, dalliance turns things upside down?

Jesus' marvelous meekness prevented any "root of bitterness" from springing up in Him (Hebrews 12:15). Ponder the Savior's precious words about the Atonement *after* He had passed through it. There is no mention of the vinegar. No mention of the scourging. No mention of having been struck. No mention of having been spat upon. He does declare that He "suffer[ed] both body and spirit" in an exquisiteness and soreness which we simply cannot comprehend. (See D&C 19:15, 18.)

We come now to the last and most terrible irony of Jesus: His feeling forsaken on Calvary at the apogee of His agony. The apparent withdrawal of the Father's Spirit then evoked the greatest soul cry in human history. (See James E. Talmage, *Jesus the Christ* [Salt Lake City: The Church of Jesus Christ of Latter-day Saints, 1916], pp. 660–61.) This deprivation had never happened to Christ before—never. Yet thereby Jesus became a fully comprehending Christ, and thus He was enabled to be a fully succoring Savior (see D&C 88:6; Alma 7:11–12). Moreover, even in the darkest hour, while feeling forsaken, Jesus submitted Himself to the Father. No wonder the Savior tells us that the combined anguish in

Gethsemane and on Calvary was so awful that He wished it were possible to shrink from drinking that bitter cup. "Nevertheless," He finished His "preparation." (See D&C 19:18-19; 3 Nephi 11:11.) The word *nevertheless* reflected deep, divine determination.

Even after treading the winepress alone (see D&C 76:107), which ended in His stunning, personal triumph and in the greatest victory ever, majestic Jesus meekly declared, "Glory be to the Father"! (D&C 19:19.) This should not surprise us. In the premortal world Jesus meekly volunteered to be our Savior, saying, "Father, thy will be done, and the glory be thine forever" (Moses 4:2). Jesus was true to His word.

"Glory be to the Father"—first, for rearing such an incomparable Son! "Glory be to the Father" for allowing His special Son to suffer and to be sacrificed for all of us! Certainly on Judgment Day none of us will want to rush forward to tell our Father how we, as parents, suffered when we watched our children suffer.

Enduring irony, though a real challenge on the way to becoming men and women of Christ, is but one dimension of the larger and regular challenge of enduring.

On one of those rare occasions when His very voice was heard, the Father testified: "Yea, the words of my Beloved are true and faithful. He that endureth to the end, the same shall be saved." (2 Nephi 31:15.) Of all that the Father might then have said, He stressed endurance. Why?

The major reason is that God has repeatedly said He would structure mortality to be a proving and testing experience (see Abraham 3:25; Mosiah 23:21). He has certainly kept His promise and carried out His divine intent. Thus even our fiery trials, said Peter, should not be thought of as "some strange thing" (1 Peter 4:12). Hence enduring is vital, and those who so last will be first spiritually! Enduring is more than lasting, however: we are to "endure it well" and to endure it "valiantly" (D&C 121:8, 29).

By taking Jesus' yoke upon us and enduring, we learn most deeply of Him and especially how to be like Him (see Matthew 11:29). Even though our experiences are micro compared to His, the process is the same.

There are many things to be endured, trials like illness, injustice, insensitivity, poverty, aloneness, unresponsiveness, being misrepresented and misunderstood, and sometimes seeing friends become enemies. Paul reminds us that meek and lowly Jesus, though the Lord of the universe, "endured . . . contradiction of sinners against himself" (Hebrews 12:3). Smaller variations of these contradictions or hostilities will be felt by His disciples.

We tend to think only in terms of our endurance, but it is God's patient long-suffering that provides us with our chances to improve, affording us urgently needed developmental space or time (see Alma 42:4–5).

Paul observed, "Now no chastening for the present seemeth to be joyous, but grievous: nevertheless afterward it yieldeth the peaceable fruit of righteousness" (Hebrews 12:11). Such peaceable fruit comes only in its appointed season, after the buds and the blossoms.

If this were not so, if certain mortal experiences were cut short, it would be like pulling up a flower to see how the roots are doing. Put another way, make too many anxious openings of the oven door and the cake falls instead of rising. Moreover, enforced change usually does not last, while productive enduring can ingrain permanent change (see Alma 32:13).

Patient endurance is to be distinguished from merely being "acted upon." Endurance is more than pacing up and down within the cell of our circumstance; it is not only acceptance of the things allotted to us but also the determination to "act for ourselves" by magnifying what is allotted to us (Alma 29:3, 6).

If, for instance, we are always taking our temperature to see whether we are happy, we will not be. If we are constantly comparing to see if things are fair, we are being unfair to ourselves.

True enduring therefore represents not merely the passage of time but also the passage of the soul — and not merely from A to B, but amid "mighty change" all the way from A to Z. To endure in faith and do God's will thus involves much more than putting up with a circumstance (see D&C 63:20; 101:35).

Rather than shoulder-shrugging, true enduring is soul trembling. Jesus bled not at a few pores but "at every pore" (D&C 19:18).

Sometimes spiritual obedience requires us to "hold on" lovingly, such as to a rebellious child, while others, despairing, cry, "Let go!" Enduring may likewise mean, however, letting go when everything within us wants to hold on, such as to a loved one "appointed unto death" (D&C 42:48).

Patient endurance permits us to cling to our faith in the Lord and our faith in His timing when we are being tossed about by the surf of circumstance. Even when a seeming undertow grasps us, somehow in the tumbling we are being carried forward, though battered and bruised.

When, for the moment, we ourselves are not being stretched on a particular cross, we ought to be at the foot of someone else's — full of empathy and proffering spiritual refreshment.

With enduring comes a willingness, therefore, to "press forward" (2 Nephi 31:20) even when we are bone weary and would much rather pull off to the side of the road. Hence, one prophet was especially commended by the Lord for his unwearyingness (see Helaman 10:4; 15:6).

Paul wrote that, even after faithful disciples had "done the will of God," they "[had] need of patience" (Hebrews 10:36). How many times have good people done the right thing initially only to break under subsequent stress? Sustaining correct conduct for a difficult moment under extraordinary stress is very commendable, but so is coping with sustained stress subtly present in seeming routineness. Either way, however, we are to "run with patience the race that is set before us" (Hebrews 12:1); and it is a marathon, not a sprint.

When you and I are unduly impatient, we like our time-table better than God's. And thus, while the scriptural phrase "in process of time" means "eventually," it also denotes an entire spiritual process: "The Lord showed unto Enoch all the inhabitants of the earth; and he beheld, and lo, Zion, in process of time, was taken up into heaven" (Moses 7:21; see also D&C 38:13; Genesis 4:3; 38:12; Exodus 2:23; Judges 11:4; 2 Chronicles 21:19).

By itself, of course, the passage of time does not bring an automatic advance. Yet, like the prodigal son, we often need the process of time in order to come to our spiritual senses (see Luke 15:17). The touching reunion of Jacob and Esau in the desert, so many years after their sibling rivalry, is a classic example. Generosity can replace animosity. But reflection and introspection require time. A great many spiritual outcomes require that saving truths be mixed with time, forming the elixir of experience, that sovereign remedy for many things.

Hence the ongoing-ness of it all. So perhaps we can be forgiven for wondering, "Is there no other way?" Indeed there is no other way, for personal, spiritual symmetry emerges only from the shaping of prolonged obedience. Twigs are bent, not snapped, into shape.

Without patient and meek endurance we will learn less, see less, feel less, and hear less. We who are egocentric and impatient shut down much of our receiving capacity.

The enlarging of the soul requires not only some re-modeling but also some excavating. Hypocrisy, guile, and other imbedded traits do not go gladly or easily, but if we "endure it well" we will not grow testy while being tested. We note too that sorrow can actually enlarge the mind and heart in order to "give place," providing expanded space for later joy.

Thus enduring is one of the cardinal attributes, but it simply cannot be developed without time or the laboratory of this second estate. All the other cardinal virtues—love,

patience, humility, mercy, purity, submissiveness, justice —
similarly require endurance for their full development.

The harrowing of the soul can be like the harrowing of
the soil; to increase the yield, things are turned upside down.
Moses experienced such topsy-turvy change. A lesser individual could not have forsaken Egypt's treasures and privi-
leged status only to be later hunted and resented as a pro-
phetic presence in the royal courts, courts which he had
doubtless known earlier as an insider. Yet we are told that
Moses, because of his esteem for Christ, endured by faith
(see Hebrews 11:24–29). As a Father, God is delighted with
our first and further steps, but He knows how straight, how
narrow, and how long the ensuing path is. Again, how vital
is endurance!

Meanwhile, with spiritual endurance we can have felicity
amid poverty, gratitude without plentitude. There can even
be meekness amid injustice. One never sees the "root of bitterness springing up" (Hebrews 12:15) in the enduring meek.
While in the midst of all these things, if we are wise like Job
we will avoid charging God foolishly (see Job 1:22).

As with every virtue, Jesus is the exemplar. While
shouldering Jesus' yoke we can better come to "know according to the flesh how to succor [each other]" (Alma 7:12).

Likewise, by seeing life's experiences on through to the
end, on our small scale we can finally say, as Jesus did on the
cross, "It is finished" (John 19:30). We too can then have
"finished [our] preparations," having done the particular
work God gave each of us to do (D&C 19:19; see also John
17:4). But our tiny cup cannot be taken from us any more
than the Savior's huge one could from Him. For this reason
we too have come into the world (see John 12:27).

In a small but nevertheless sufficient way we will experience what it is to suffer "both body and spirit" (see D&C
19:18). Some afflictions are physical, others mental, or they
begin so. Often, however, they are interactive in both areas,
forming a special pain.

One of the most powerful and searching questions ever asked of all of us in our sufferings hangs in time and space before us: "The Son of Man hath descended below them all. Art thou greater than he?" (D&C 122:8.) Jesus both plumbed the depths and scaled the heights in order to comprehend all things (see D&C 88:6). Jesus therefore is not only a fully atoning but also a fully comprehending Savior!

Included in the challenge of enduring is enduring the process of being improved. Remodeling is always costly and painful. How can putting off the old man and putting on the new man be otherwise?

CHAPTER 6

"In a Preparation"

There can be no improvement without positive change and without our also enduring the preparatory things. It is therefore wise for us to ponder what especially facilitates such positive change; and further, what we can do to take advantage of and even create the "in a preparation" moments.

Though spiritual improvement is usually gradual, clearly there are pivotal moments. These shining moments, if used before time tarnishes them, can bless us and others significantly. While some of these involve us personally, sometimes we can, in the words of the resurrected Jesus, become "the means of bringing salvation unto" other individuals (see 3 Nephi 18:32).

Whether in any instance we would be helpers or would be helped, humbly invoking the presence of the Spirit is vital. We are clearly not wise enough to manage things by ourselves (see Alma 31:34, 35). The Holy Ghost, however, can tell us "all things what [we] should do" (2 Nephi 32:3, 5). The help of the Spirit is especially needed when we are being enrolled in a spiritual seminar for which we did not sign up! The Spirit not only gives us much needed access to "God's files" but also customizes the counsel flowing from these files.

As individuals we are at risk if we "seek to counsel in [our] own ways" (D&C 56:14), drawing only upon the limited framework of our experience. For instance, we cannot always judge wisely until the Lord makes certain things known to us: "But as you cannot always judge the righteous, or as you cannot always tell the wicked from the righteous, therefore I say unto you, hold your peace until I shall see fit to make all things known unto the world concerning the matter" (D&C 10:37). Wheat and tares can look so much alike to the untutored and undiscerning eye.

The resurrected Jesus similarly counseled leaders in the Nephite society not to give up impatiently on the lost sheep, for "ye know not but what they will return and repent" (3 Nephi 18:32). Because we are not fully able to know the hearts of others without help from the Lord, the role of the Spirit is crucial.

The presence of some divine discontent or dissonance in our lives or in the lives of others is another facilitating factor. The Lord has often so "arranged" things that we find individuals already "in a preparation to hear the word" (Alma 32:6). For instance, sorrow can be a facilitator; as one of many ways in which life's terrain can be shaken it can prepare the mind and heart and stir us to pondering. Deeply despondent as sorrow may make us, however, self-pity is not the same thing as godly sorrow. Soaking in the hot tub of self-pity does not do for us what godly sorrow does — namely, brace us! Godly sorrow is like going from a sauna into a snowbank; it produces a tingly, spiritual stimulation. Unchallenged lukewarmness and apathy, on the other hand, leave little room for bringing about improvement: "I would thou wert cold or hot," the Lord said (Revelation 3:15). Dissonance has its dangers, but apathy surely does not bring about "a desire to believe."

Just as there is "faith unto repentance" (Alma 34:15) there is likewise real sorrow that works true repentance (Mormon 2:13–14).

In contrast there is the "sorrowing of the damned," which occurs when people can no longer have it both ways; they can no longer take happiness in sin, and yet they remain unrescued because they have not turned completely to God (see Mormon 2:12–14).

Some breakthroughs toward positive change are immediate, as on the day of Pentecost in ancient Jerusalem: "Now when they heard this, they were pricked in their heart, and said unto Peter and to the rest of the apostles, Men and brethren, what shall we do?" (Acts 2:37.)

Some insights are sudden if we catch hold of them, as in Alma's dramatic conversion:

> And it came to pass that as I was thus racked with torment, while I was harrowed up by the memory of my many sins, behold, I remembered also to have heard my father prophesy unto the people concerning the coming of one Jesus Christ, a Son of God, to atone for the sins of the world.
>
> Now, as my mind caught hold upon this thought, I cried within my heart: O Jesus, thou Son of God, have mercy on me, who am in the gall of bitterness, and am encircled about by the everlasting chains of death. (Alma 36:17–18.)

At other times "preparation to hear the word" is gradual, finally cresting in a moment of decision — as with the prodigal son: "And when he came to himself, he said, How many hired servants of my father's have bread enough and to spare, and I perish with hunger! I will arise and go to my father, and will say unto him, Father, I have sinned against heaven, and before thee." (Luke 15:17–18.)

The Lord can commence His initial work with us while requiring surprisingly little from us. Alma explained: "But behold, if ye will awake and arouse your faculties, even to an experiment upon my words, and exercise a particle of faith, yea, even if ye can no more than desire to believe, let this desire work in you, even until ye believe in a manner that ye can give place for a portion of my words" (Alma 32:27).

Imagine, only "a particle of faith" and "no more than [a] desire to believe" are actually enough to begin!

Golden questions also can create golden moments of truth. Framing the moment of truth with directness and loving concern can be very helpful.

It may be well, at the right time, to pose today's equivalents of these questions: "What have you against being baptized [or becoming active]?" (Mosiah 18:10) and "If ye have felt to sing the song of redeeming love, . . . can ye feel so now?" (Alma 5:26.) In this way we can help righteous and responsive nostalgia to play a real role.

"If thou canst believe. . . ." said Jesus. The anxious but honest father replied: "I believe; help thou mine unbelief." (Mark 9:23–24.)

Inspired questions not only elicit helpful comments but also assist us in determining the individual's existing degree of doctrinal or spiritual knowledge. Former-day examples are: "He said unto them, Have ye received the Holy Ghost since ye believed? And they said unto him, We have not so much as heard whether there be any Holy Ghost." (Acts 19:2.) "Have ye received his image in your countenances?" (Alma 5:14.)

"What place does Jesus have in your life now?" is a good question in this context. When people have been "in a preparation" and when the Spirit is present, meek, intellectual integrity is likely.

And Aaron answered him and said unto him: Believest thou that there is a God? And the king said: I know that the Amalekites say that there is a God, and I have granted unto them that they should build sanctuaries, that they may assemble themselves together to worship him. And if now thou sayest there is a God, behold I will believe.

This spiritual surrender led to the king's first attempt at prayer:

> O God, Aaron hath told me that there is a God; and if there is a God, and if thou art God, wilt thou make thyself known unto me, and I will give away all my sins to know thee, and that I may be raised from the dead, and be saved at the last day. (Alma 22:7, 18.)

We may also ask questions to get on-the-record responses rather than information, as in "Whom say ye that I am?" (Matthew 16:15.) On occasion, questions may even elicit questions to which, finally, resounding response may be given: "Saul, Saul, why persecutest thou me?" "Who art thou, Lord?" "I am Jesus." (Acts 9:4–5.)

Questions may be tutorial, as with the brother of Jared: "What will ye that I should do that ye may have light in your vessels? For behold, ye cannot have windows, neither . . . fire." (Ether 2:23.)

In any case, the power of inspired words is great indeed.

> The word had a . . . more powerful effect upon the minds of the people than . . . anything else (Alma 31:5).

> And if now thou sayest there is a God, behold I will believe (Alma 22:7).

> Blessed art thou . . . because of thy exceeding faith in the words alone of my servant (Mosiah 26:15, 16).

> And again, more blessed are they who shall believe in your words because that ye shall testify that ye have seen me, and that ye know that I am. Yea, blessed are they who shall believe in your words, and come down into the depths of humility and be baptized, for they shall be visited with fire and with the Holy Ghost, and shall receive a remission of their sins. (3 Nephi 12:2.)

> And Ammon said unto her: Believest thou this? And she said unto him: I have had no witness save thy word, and

the word of our servants; nevertheless I believe that it shall
be according as thou hast said. (Alma 19:9.)

And many of the Samaritans of that city believed on him
for the saying of the woman, which testified, He told me all
that ever I did (John 4:39).

Valued and saving as the words of others are, having
one's own personal witness is still to be preferred.

So when the Samaritans were come unto him, they be-
sought him that he would tarry with them: and he abode
there two days.
And many more believed because of his own word;
And said unto the woman, Now we believe, not because
of thy saying: for we have heard him ourselves, and know
that this is indeed the Christ, the Savior of the world. (John
4:40–42.)

To some it is given by the Holy Ghost to know that
Jesus Christ is the Son of God, and that he was crucified for
the sins of the world.
To others it is given to believe on their words, that they
also might have eternal life if they continue faithful. (D&C
46:13–14.)

The Holy Ghost so teaches us that spiritual truths are
helpfully connected with each other:

And now, my beloved brethren, and also Jew, and all ye
ends of the earth, hearken unto these words and believe in
Christ; and if ye believe not in these words believe in
Christ. And if ye shall believe in Christ ye will believe in
these words, for they are the words of Christ, and he hath
given them unto me; and they teach all men that they
should do good. (2 Nephi 33:10.)

The Lord can compensate for our communication weaknesses. Nephi wrote: "And the words which I have written in
weakness will be made strong unto them." What key things

did he convey? "For it *persuadeth them to do good;* it *maketh known unto them of their fathers;* and it *speaketh of Jesus,* and *persuadeth them to believe in him,* and to *endure to the end"* (2 Nephi 33:4, italics added).

Nephi had a preferred way of communicating: "Neither am I [Nephi] mighty in writing, like unto speaking; for when a man speaketh by the power of the Holy Ghost the power of the Holy Ghost carrieth it unto the hearts of the children of men" (2 Nephi 33:1).

Yet, as Joseph Smith learned by his 1820 experience, and in ways which have benefitted millions, the Holy Ghost powerfully endorses the Lord's written word too: "If any of you lack wisdom, let him ask of God, that giveth to all men liberally, and upbraideth not; and it shall be given him" (James 1:5).

Whether in writing or by the spoken word, "he that receiveth the word by the Spirit of truth receiveth it as it is preached by the Spirit of truth. Wherefore, he that preacheth and he that receiveth, understand one another, and both are edified and rejoice together." (D&C 50:21–22.)

On occasion, these golden times involve moments of spiritual stillness that is more than the absence of sound. Rather, it is a stillness which focuses us, and we feel it. This stillness subdues the soul, bringing as it were the powerful presence of something else, something superior. Yet this powerful presence is unforced; in fact, it will flee before doubt or resistance; it can quickly be driven out by disdain. In these moments of stillness we learn by inspiration and even revelation.

In summation, golden moments happen in many ways and in many situations. They are caused and furthered under direction of the Spirit. Such moments are usually framed in "a tiny moment" of time but involve all eternity! Such moments usually involve directness and candidness in both questions and answers.

Even if not pursued, at least such moments can produce an on-the-record response, as with King Agrippa: "Almost thou persuadest me" (Acts 26:28).

Few experiences produce such positive change as do full-time missions. Without attempting to be exhaustive or definitive, one may suggest reasons why full-time missions usually are such a significant period of spiritual progress.

Dedicated full-time missionaries have fewer distractions in their lives. They are serving others intensively and in a known, compressed time frame, working against the clock while serving the purposes of eternity. In the missionary environment there is usually more consistent self-discipline than at home. There is the wise and regularized "overseership" of a mission president. There is usually the presence of a reminding and reinforcing companion. Missionaries usually live closer to the Lord through regular prayer and by searching His scriptures. There is more stretching of the self in their service because more is specifically required, such as in the development of empathy and interest in others even if such feelings are unreciprocated. The missionaries usually honor the formula for faith and study, service, prayers, and worship.

Conversely, why is it that so often "at home," even with good parents and Church activity, we do not necessarily see similar spiritual progress? First, at home our youth are more inclined to focus on self, though some of this is understandably needed since career choices are to be pursued and a wise selection of an eternal companion is to be made. At home too there is often more pleasing of oneself and less structure and less self-discipline than in the mission field. Furthermore, service at home is often limited mainly to one's formal Church calling, a part-time thing at best.

In addition, the young person at home lacks a full-time companion to encourage the personal development. He usually does less daily scripture study. And too little that is really meaningful in getting young persons outside the tiny theater of self-concern is required by loving parents and leaders, though it need not be so.

The contrasts — some unavoidable — are worth thinking about. Generally the remarkable growth we often see as a result of full-time missions dwarfs the more "slack" yield we frequently see at home.

It is clear that the possibilities for greater positive change are enormous for all of us at home! They lie all around us! There is so much to do and so little time, and so few golden teaching moments.

Inasmuch as we can "be the means of bringing salvation" to others, we should each consider the following questions: What is our *doctrinal* impact on those we serve or influence? What is our *personal* impact on those we serve or influence? What is our *training* impact on those we serve or influence? Or is our influence non-specific and merely marginal?

It may be that what is needed is to remonstrate or reassure, correct or commend, verify or clarify, counsel or listen, and so forth.

If reproving counsel is needed, we are to show an increase in love after administering the reproof (D&C 121:43). Brigham Young said that we should not chasten beyond the capacity of our healing balm (see *Journal of Discourses* 9:124–25). Paul said we are also to comfort and to forgive, lest the errant one "be swallowed up with overmuch sorrow" (2 Corinthians 2:7).

Much helping is likewise accomplished through appreciation, encouragement, commendation, reassurance, and variations of "You can do it!" In this way horizons are expanded, precious perspective is provided:

> And the night following the Lord stood by him, and said, Be of good cheer, Paul: for as thou hast testified of me in Jerusalem, so must thou bear witness also at Rome (Acts 23:11).

> The ends of the earth shall inquire after thy name, and fools shall have thee in derision, and hell shall rage against thee (D&C 122:1).

> And when Enoch had heard these words, he bowed himself to the earth, before the Lord, and spake before the

Lord, saying: Why is it that I have found favor in thy sight, and am but a lad, and all the people hate me; for I am slow of speech; wherefore am I thy servant?

And the Lord said unto Enoch: Go forth and do as I have commanded thee, and no man shall pierce thee. Open thy mouth, and it shall be filled, and I will give thee utterance, for all flesh is in my hands, and I will do as seemeth me good.

Say unto this people: Choose ye this day, to serve the Lord God who made you. (Moses 6:31–33.)

Now the Lord had shown unto me, Abraham, the intelligences that were organized before the world was; and among all these there were many of the noble and great ones;

And God saw these souls that they were good, and he stood in the midst of them, and he said: These I will make my rulers; for he stood among those that were spirits, and he saw that they were good; and he said unto me: Abraham, thou art one of them; thou wast chosen before thou wast born (Abraham 3:22–23).

Before I formed thee in the belly I knew thee; and before thou camest forth out of the womb I sanctified thee, and I ordained thee a prophet unto the nations (Jeremiah 1:5).

The sometimes stern Duke of Wellington, in the sunset of his life, was asked how he could do better if he were to live his life over again. Said he, "I should have given more praise" (Elizabeth Longford, *Wellington: The Years of the Sword* [New York: Harper and Row, 1969], p. 486). How many of us display that same deficiency?

Helping also includes showing "how," teaching specific doctrines, clarifying the problem, and bringing a fresh view, as in the divine help given the brother of Jared regarding building barges (see Ether 2:16 to 3:5).

The Prophet Joseph Smith emphasized the importance of our understanding the character of God, one of whose attributes is love.

Love is one of the chief characteristics of Deity, and ought to be manifested by those who aspire to be the sons of God. A man filled with the love of God, is not content with blessing his family alone, but ranges through the whole world, anxious to bless the whole human race. (*Teachings of the Prophet Joseph Smith*, p. 174.)

There are but very few beings in the world who understand rightly the character of God. The great majority of mankind do not comprehend anything, either that which is past or that which is to come, as it respects their relationship to God. They do not know, neither do they understand the nature of that relationship; and consequently they know but little, . . . more than to eat, drink, and sleep. This is all man knows about God or his existence, unless it is given by the inspiration of the Almighty. . . . If men do not comprehend the character of God, they do not comprehend themselves. (*Teachings*, p. 343.)

It is the first principle of the Gospel to know for a certainty the Character of God. (*Teachings*, p. 345.)

When we understand the character of God, and know how to come to him, he begins to unfold the heavens to us, and to tell us all about it. When we are ready to come to him, he is ready to come to us. (*Teachings*, p. 350.)

While we may crave dramatic change and sudden improvement, most often this progress will be gradual. Therefore we should come to value the small things that make up such a large share of the Lord's large blessings.

CHAPTER 7

"Things As They Really Are"

Often, becoming men and women of Christ involves seemingly micro-movement on our part. We surely see God's guidance in the small, personal things as well as in the larger and spectacular things. There is guiding revelation in the slightest divine inflection. After all, divine tutoring occurs not only massively but incrementally — "line upon line, precept upon precept" (see Isaiah 28:10; D&C 98:12).

The parting of the Red Sea was certainly spectacular, but those roiling waters soon resumed their more placid place. In the perspective of eternity, was that dramatic parting any greater than God's gradually opening the way for a reconciliation between Esau and Jacob? or His dramatically opening the curtains of Peter's understanding to envision that Christ's gospel was for Gentiles as well as for Israel?

Day in and day out the same Lord who parted the Red Sea so that Israel might escape Egypt provides ways for us to escape temptation (see 1 Corinthians 10:13). "By very small means," Alma told his son, "the Lord . . . bringeth about the salvation of many souls" (Alma 37:7). Scale, therefore, is not the sole measure of spiritual significance; for "out of small things proceedeth that which is great" (D&C 64:33).

Whether in geologic convulsion or in geologic gradualism, God once parted the continents and oceans (see Genesis 10:25; D&C 133:24). He can also part the curtains of our individual understanding by helping us see "things as they really are" (Jacob 4:13). Has He not said He will guide us by His being on our left and right hands, showing us the way, disclosing "here a little, and there a little"? (D&C 128:21; see also 84:88.)

A marvelous insight is given to us by the brother of Jared, who observed that even when the Lord shows "forth great power" it can, ironically, nevertheless look "small unto the understanding of men" (Ether 3:5). The natural eye not only misses the small things of the Lord but also misjudges them as to source. This is an enormously important clue in understanding the ways of the Lord, which are higher than man's ways (see Isaiah 55:8). We think of God's power as being massive and galactic, and it is; but often it is expressed in small ways, and hence its significance is misread by mortals. Could it be that the higher ways of God consist partly of His competency in His expansive effectiveness but also in micro matters? Indeed!

When the special phrase about seeing things "as they really are" is employed, it brings to mind the episode of the young man who served with the prophet Elisha. They were encompassed about with enemy chariots. Understandably alarmed, the young man said, "Master! how shall we do?" Elisha, hoping to comfort the young man, responded, "Fear not: for they that be with us are more than they that be with them." To the natural eye, this clearly was not the case; the forces of righteousness were obviously outnumbered by those of their enemy. So the prophet prayed for the young man that his eyes might be opened, that he, too, might see. Then came the great blessing: "The Lord opened the eyes of the young man; and he saw: and, behold, the mountain was full of horses and chariots of fire." (See 2 Kings 6:13–17.)

It is that process of enlightenment that is vital. We cannot fully or clearly see with the natural eye. It is too uncurious, too myopic, too interested in nonspiritual things. But with the eye of faith we can truly see things as they really are.

If we are meek, God can guide our smallest steps, leading us into needed light or deflecting us from a seemingly small misstep, such as a temptation that incrementally might alter our life's course. He can inspire us to hold fast when our weary grip yearns to relax.

In the miracle of the loaves and the fishes many of those benefitted were doubtless hungry again the very next day. Is the miracle of the manna greater than the miracle of forgiveness? The miracle of the Restoration brings to us the fulness of the Bread of Life, so that we need "never hunger" (John 6:35). Jesus Himself observed that those who ate the miraculous manna were long since dead. They would have remained so, too, except for the miracle of Christ's atonement and the resurrection.

God is certainly present in the dramatic, spiritual "about faces," such as occurred on the road to Damascus, but He is also in the smaller course corrections. He surely helps the willing prodigals come to themselves, but just as surely and significantly He also steadies the unstraying who quietly and faithfully do their duties, season after season, without the recognition and celebration of the "fatted calf" (see Luke 15:11–32).

The glory God promises us is beyond our imagination — "eye hath not seen nor ear heard. . . ." (1 Corinthians 2:9.) Those who know not "the dealings of that God who . . . created them," however, thus refuse to see or to believe the big picture (1 Nephi 2:12). Lacking this precious perspective about God's "doings in other lands" (1 Nephi 19:22), they say "it is not reasonable that such a being as a Christ shall come." Furthermore, they exclaim, why doesn't He show himself to us? (Helaman 16:18.)

Some worried much about how Moses "ruled over" them (Numbers 16:13), even after the miracle of the parting of the Red Sea. But no aspirants had sought to take charge on the day when Pharaoh's armies drew menacingly close. Small minds forget large blessings! Proud minds ceaselessly inquire of God, "What have you done for me lately?"

If one is without the faith that remembers, past benefactions are forgotten because of present deprivations. Thirst for water caused some to forget that they were once rescued from far too much water at the Red Sea. It is ironical that the very repetition of some blessings can routinize these blessings. The ration of the daily miracle of manna was taken for granted, even complained about by some.

It is therefore not surprising that miracles, by themselves, neither create faith nor sustain it. For the meek and faithful, however, miracles—including blessings large and small— add to their gratitude and wonder. Far from feeling entitled, they feel overwhelmed at God's continuing goodness, graciousness, and mercy! Thus in small and various ways God leads the meek in a course across the gulf of misery and lands them safely on the other side (see Helaman 3:29–30).

Jesus, the strict Lord of the "narrow gate and the needle's eye," is also generous Jesus, He who waits for the repentant "with open arms" (Mormon 6:17). In Him is both divine exactness and divine receptiveness, both divine scrutiny and divine generosity.

The Lord's greatness is seen in the expansiveness of His works as well as in their intricacies. They reflect overwhelming vastness and also incredible personal-ness. There is stunning majesty and beauty in the handiwork of the heavens (D&C 88:47), likewise in the intricacy and beauty of the "arrayed" lilies of the field (Matthew 6:29), and in the reported double-helical symmetry of the DNA molecule (see Elizabeth L. Newhouse, ed., *Inventors and Discoverers: Changing Our World* [Washington, D.C.: National Geographic Society,

1988], p. 292). Indeed, "all things bear record of [God]" (Moses 6:63).

There are both macro- and micro-miracles (see Alma 37:41). The heavens surely witness God's majesty (D&C 88:47), but no more so than in His softening of the hard human heart.

How big is God's work of which we are part?

How large the Church will become on this earth we do not know, but the Lord has said He wants His spiritual army to become "very great." He also wants it to become "sanctified." (See D&C 105:31.) Obviously we look to spiritual as well as numerical growth, but we are probably talking about attaining Church membership of tens of millions living on this side of the veil, among earth's population, currently five-plus billion.

In addition there is the vast redemptive work in the spirit world. Demographers estimate that some 60 to 70 billion people have lived on this planet thus far. How extensive the work in the spirit world is we do not know, but it too is likely to number in the millions of converts.

As if all this were not overwhelming enough, the Lord told Moses, "but only an account of this earth, and the inhabitants thereof, give I unto you" (Moses 1:35). We know little of the Lord's work beyond what we have been told about this planet, but its vastness is strongly indicated: "That by him, and through him, and of him, the worlds are and were created, and the inhabitants thereof are begotten sons and daughters unto God" (D&C 76:24).

Thus the work of the Lord is breathtaking in its scope! We have only glimpses and scriptural inklings—enough to know we do not worship a one-planet God!

Yet despite all the universe's vastness it is also characterized by its moving personal-ness! Enoch, who was permitted to see much, exclaimed to the Lord, "Yet thou art there" (Moses 7:30).

It would be unwise, of course, for the Church to tie itself to the provisional truths of science at any point in science's unfolding history. Ultimately, scientific truth will align with divinely revealed truth; meanwhile we can applaud genuine scientific advances, noting them without depending overly much upon them. In that perspective, the following observations, quotations, and comparisons are offered.

As to divine design in the universe, a prophet was told, "worlds without number have I created" (Moses 1:33). Today,

> Astronomers in Cambridge, Mass., say they have discovered the largest structure ever seen in the universe, a collection of galaxies so extensive that it defies explanation by any present theory.
>
> Dubbed the "Great Wall," the galaxies form a sheet at least 500 million light years long, or 3,000 billion billion miles.
>
> The Great Wall's estimated length, at 500 million light years, defies almost any standard of comparison. Earth's own galaxy, the Milky Way, is only 100,000 light years across. . . . "We keep being surprised that we keep seeing something bigger as we go out farther." (David L. Chandler, "Largest Structure Found in Universe Defies Explanation," *Sacramento Union*, November 19, 1989, p. 22.)

The vastness confirms God's declaration, "There is no end to my works" (Moses 1:38).

Divine design denotes order among the planets. The Lord revealed to Abraham that another celestial body "governs all these which belong to the same order as that upon which thou standest" (Abraham 3:1–3, 4). Indeed, Kolob stands above the earth.

Meanwhile, independent of such revelations, some scientists say that

> part of the cosmos looks more like a regularly patterned honeycomb than a random explosion of matter. . . . Vast galaxies apparently are clustered in a regularly spaced pattern. (Stephen Strauss, *Globe and Mail*, February 5, 1990.)

Revelations teach that in creating this planet the Gods said, "There is space there . . . and we will make an earth" (Abraham 3:24). One astrophysicist believes the 12 other Great Walls of galaxies have roughly the same thickness. Our galaxy, the Milky Way, is located in one of the relatively empty spaces between the Great Walls. (Stephen Strauss, *Globe and Mail*, February 5, 1990.)

Within this breathtaking and precious perspective about macro and micro things, let us examine the challenges of daily life and how better to keep these in proportion as we strive to perfect what is lacking in our faith; for it is faith that moves us to action — to our emulation of Jesus.

CHAPTER 8

"Perfect That Which Is Lacking in Your Faith"

All that Jesus does by way of teaching and exemplifying for his disciples is designed to increase our faith. The meridian disciples were surely aware of their need. After the Master taught them a particularly difficult doctrine, the need for repeated forgiveness, "the apostles said unto the Lord, Increase our faith" (Luke 17:5).

We are to "walk by faith, not by sight" (2 Corinthians 5:7). Also, we are to "overcome by faith" (D&C 76:53). Yet, as Paul declared, we can live with confidence, because faith provides "the evidence of things not seen" (Hebrews 11:1). It is real evidence, but because it is of a special type many mortals dismiss it, for "the natural man receiveth not the things of the Spirit of God: for they are foolishness unto him: neither can he know them, because they are spiritually discerned" (1 Corinthians 2:14).

Powerful and centered in truth as it is, "faith is not to

have a perfect knowledge of things; therefore if ye have faith ye hope for things which are not seen, which are true" (Alma 32:21).

There can be no spiritual faith, however, that "stands in the wisdom of men" (1 Corinthians 2:5).

Enos was commended for having faith in Jesus, whom he had not then seen (see Enos 1:8). As with so many faithful disciples after their faith has been tried, Enos found that "greater things [were] made manifest" (3 Nephi 26:9). So did the once-reproved but carefully tutored and commended brother of Jared: "And because of the knowledge of this man he could not be kept from beholding within the veil; and he saw the finger of Jesus, which, when he saw, he fell with fear; for he knew that it was the finger of the Lord; and he had faith no longer, for he knew, nothing doubting" (Ether 3:19).

We are children, children who "have not as yet understood how great blessings the Father hath . . . prepared for [us]" (D&C 78:17). However, He will lead us along. He will be in our midst even though we cannot bear all things now (see D&C 78:18; 32:3; 50:40). The more we become men and women of Christ, the more we can bear, and hear, and do!

Great faith, born of doing simple things, is the key to much that matters. When we give place in our lives for developing such faith, this faith facilitates the development of other vital qualities and outcomes as well.

First, we must have sufficient "faith unto repentance" (Alma 34:15). Faith helps us to put our lives in order; without it we simply would not bother. Successful repentance then produces more faith.

No wonder that in our time of little faith the love of many in the world waxes cold (see Matthew 24:12). Faith always companies with charity and hope, qualities likewise greatly needed in times of despair (see 1 Corinthians 13:13; D&C 4:5). There is similar interplay between faith and patience (see D&C 6:19). In a pushy, selfish world, how vital patience is in deferring certain gratifications, lest in our "me-ness" and "now-ness" we go on, for instance, placing our grandchildren more deeply in debt!

True faith will also lead to good works, of which there is surely no surplus. Ponder how much human deprivation and discouragement result from the scarcity of good works arising from a scarcity of faith! (See James 2:14.)

To our faith we will add virtue, which will help us to be portable lights to the world (Philippians 2:15).

Little wonder, therefore, that faith is the *first principle* of the gospel of Jesus Christ! It is no surprise that this first principle is so clearly, obviously, and necessarily connected with the first great commandment—to love God with all our strength, mind, and soul.

As essential as faith is, it is strange that we should stumble so often over how to increase it. Why should we be so slow to discern specifically what is lacking to keep us from strengthening our faith? (See 1 Thessalonians 3:10.) The simple remedies for increasing our faith lie within easy reach.

To supply what is lacking in our faith we must first make room for its conscious development—in our souls and in our schedules.

What happens after we really "give place" for the gospel in our lives? It is analogous to a seed that begins to "swell," "fill," and "enlarge [one's] soul," and " to enlighten [one's] understanding." Of the results of such verifiable outcomes, asked Alma, "Would not this increase your faith?" (Alma 32:28-29.) He continued, observing that the seed "swelleth," and "sprouteth," asking, "behold, will not this strengthen your faith?" Through this process of personal verification we can, accurately and experientially, come to say, "I know that this is a good seed," and thus faith yields to knowledge "in that thing" (Alma 32:30, 34). But we cannot have the results of the experiment without performing the experiment. Some of us "give" only postage stamp "place" in our lives, and yet we expect the yield of an acre! "Place" means time, thought, and service.

In the process of building faith, wrote Alma, we must

"experiment on the word" of the Master, giving "place" sufficient to experiment upon each essential "thing" the gospel requires of us. Out of such cumulative experience comes the real, cumulative evidence.

Nevertheless, inquirers after more faith are often disappointed or are put off when told to "study, serve, pray, and worship." They expect to hear something else, something more. As with Naaman, a reminder is needed: "If the prophet had bid thee do some great thing, wouldest thou not have done it?" (2 Kings 5:13.)

As we speak in terms of worshipping, serving, studying, and praying, we perceive that there are many implications attached to those well-worn words. Certainly by serving we hasten the shedding of selfishness and quicken our commitment to the second great commandment. Likewise, studying facilitates our remembering—not only do we recall the things out of our personal lives but also we have placed before us the enlarged memory of holy scriptures with all of the relevant accounts out of mankind's spiritual history (Alma 37:8). More important, by studying we come to know God the Eternal Father and His Son Jesus Christ. Not only is this essential to life eternal; also it gives us a symmetry as between things intellectual and spiritual.

By praying, we begin to experience what it is like when we see the interplay of man's moral agency and God's directing hand. These are things to be learned only by experience. We learn how important our intentions are, since we are instructed to pray for that "which is right" (3 Nephi 18:20). Our prayers will be better if they are in fact inspired prayers.

Thus worshipping, serving, studying, praying, each in its own way squeezes selfishness out of us; it pushes aside our preoccupations with the things of the world.

Our objective, of course, is to increase our faith in the Lord, in His plan, in His timing, and in His love. Studying helps us push forward the borders of our understanding, revealing God in His fulness and inspiring awe in us as we understand that He truly is able to do His own work (see 2 Nephi 27:20–21). As we serve, by magnifying our calling, including practicing "pure religion and undefiled" (James 1:27), we gain experience in appreciating all that God has done for us and what taking His yoke upon us truly does to help us learn of Him.

From our own experiences—worshipping, serving, praying, and studying—we learn not only that God is actually there but also that He is truly worthy of our total trust and full faith. Moreover, we see how He delivers on His promises, and this equips us to face further challenges. The young Nephi had reached that point: "And it came to pass that I, Nephi, said unto my father: I will go and do the things which the Lord hath commanded, for I know that the Lord giveth no commandments unto the children of men, save he shall prepare a way for them that they may accomplish the thing which he commandeth them" (1 Nephi 3:7).

Possessed of faith, we need not understand all things all at once in order to know the most basic things: "I know that [God] loveth his children; nevertheless, I do not know the meaning of all things" (1 Nephi 11:17).

Thus faith is experiential, producing "evidence of things not seen" but which are nevertheless true (Hebrews 11:1). As the Lord cumulatively reveals Himself to us, this enables "the mind of man to place confidence in Him without reservation" ("Faith," LDS Bible Dictionary, p. 669). Therefore, obeying and learning go together—just as do studying and serving.

When Paul wrote of his desire to help members at Thessalonica "perfect that which [was] lacking in [their] faith" (1 Thessalonians 3:10), later in the epistle he wrote of their need to serve and to love one another, to "pray without ceasing," to "despise not prophesyings," and to be more holy and pure. He also taught them of the resurrection and Christ's second coming. Did the members at Thessalonica thereafter "give place" for Paul's words? Did they "experiment upon" Paul's words and do the simple things "commanded"? The opportunity was there to increase their faith, but was it heeded?

To "come unto Christ, and be perfected in Him" (Moroni 10:32) means moving toward Him, becoming more like Him, step by step. Delaying will not lessen the vast distance to be traveled. Procrastinating will not bring the emergence of new alternatives. All the anxiety and energy expended in milling about does not move us one inch forward on the path of discipleship. (See Joel 3:14.)

At the center of what is lacking is usually the reluctance to choose, or to "give place," or to get started, or to resume the journey. We should choose, for refusing to choose is actually a decision as between life's two fundamental alternatives: "Wherefore, men are free. . . . to choose liberty and eternal life, through the great Mediator of all men, or to choose captivity and death, according to the captivity and power of the devil; for he seeketh that all men might be miserable like unto himself." (2 Nephi 2:27; see also Alma 3:26; 41:11.)

Without realizing the inherent inconsistency, some want happiness along with worldliness—which cannot be (see Alma 41:10). We "are free to choose," and choose we will, either subtly or dramatically. But the alternatives and consequences will not change.

The Lord clearly recognizes that not all have faith: "And as all have not faith, seek ye diligently and teach one another words of wisdom; yea, seek ye out of the best books words of wisdom; seek learning, even by study and also by faith" (D&C 88:118).

There must be the hearing of the word, because faith comes by that hearing (Romans 10:17). But hearing, by itself, is not always enough. Some individuals, even when so informed, may not acknowledge the "dealings of the God who [has] created them" (1 Nephi 2:12; Mosiah 10:14) or His "doings" elsewhere and with other peoples (1 Nephi 19:22; Helaman 16:19, 20).

Doing all this requires some time and the genuine focusing of attention. If we are too busy or too lazy, or too inconsistent in our efforts, we have given place to other things.

No wonder the scriptures say the time will come when "they that murmured shall learn doctrine" (Isaiah 29:24). At that time, they shall learn about things "as they really are" (Jacob 4:13).

Jesus asks us to "doubt not"—to give place attitudinally so that what at first may appear to be only a possibility can next become a probability and then a reality. To receive His work with a doubtful or slothful heart is to skew the experiment; either no place or insufficient place is given (see Matthew 21:21). These individuals have actually decided before they have truly and fully experimented. True disciples are initiators willing to cross developmental lines, for "he will give unto the faithful line upon line, precept upon precept" (D&C 98:12). These are they who "overcome by faith" (D&C 76:53). One promise is: "I will tell you in your mind" (D&C 8:2). Yes, such whisperings are "spiritually discerned." Yes, these lie outside the hearing of others. But they are audible to the disciple who has ears to hear.

Spiritual experiences provide repeated verifications, telling us again and again what we already know. Life even seems geared to repeat certain lessons. However, unremembered experiences cannot help us. Hence having a poor spiritual memory diminishes discipleship.

Better to walk by faith and receive its quiet evidence of things not seen than to see extraordinary things and then stumble over but ordinary challenges.

Similarly, disputes over milk or over a misspelled name in a revelation, murmuring over minor imperfections in Joseph Smith, concern over getting more credit, and so on, have all combined in the past to overcome other individuals in one degree or another. At this historical distance we may think, "How silly!" But without meekness, faith is vulnerable; and for pride, nothing is too petty to be seized upon.

Faith can falter when some of those who have played significant roles in the past feel left out later on as this great work moves on. From his jail cell even the great prophet

John the Baptist sought reassurance (see Luke 7:19-23). Lack of mortal appreciation for past performances can occur. It did when there arose in Egypt a new king "which knew not Joseph" (Exodus 1:8). Yet Joseph had done so much and so admirably, including helping to feed thousands of Egyptians.

When what we personally have contributed in the past is now less noticed, if we are not meek we may notice more the imperfections of current leaders. As we cease giving place we "neglect the tree," and the "heat of the sun . . . scorcheth it" (Alma 32:37, 38). The meek, however, even in disappointment, will continue to nurture the tree of testimony by worship, service, study, and prayer.

Oliver Cowdery's readmission to the Church—tender, humble, and sweet—is a reminder of how, as we can understand, even then he wanted people to know he had played a leading part in the beginnings of this great work, as he surely did.

High status and unusual spiritual experiences are not guarantees of spiritual survival. These may even bring extra burdens. Regardless of our station, however, the yoke is easy to bear at any stage—but only if we are meek and lowly. It takes meekness to give place and to continue to give place for the nurturing and nourishing of faith to develop what we lack.

As we worship God with all of our mind, soul, and strength we move from appreciation to adoration and on to emulation. Our minds are involved in studying and pondering. Our souls are extended in service. Finally we reach a consecration of all things.

To be passed over can be wrongly construed as being unvalued by God or by one's colleagues. Yet in the kingdom of God to be *uncalled* is clearly not to be *unworthy,* or *unable!* The meek understand this. Hyrum Smith never worried that younger Joseph, in a sense, "ruled over him." No wonder the Lord praised Hyrum for the integrity of his heart. The man or woman of Christ is not easily offended.

If we do not remember how "we have proved [God] in days that are past," then the experimental evidence can be lost. Hence going through the files of faith, counting our blessings, is needed. It aids intellectual honesty and serves as an internal auditing.

The cardinal virtues, including faith, are all necessary for overcoming this world but are all likewise essential for happy survival in the next world. Since faith helped frame the universe and since "faith . . . is the moving cause of all action" (*Lectures on Faith* 1:10), how would one fare amidst the galaxies and eternities without faith?

How could one assist the Lord's work in the world to come without having learned, here and now, obedience to the laws upon which all blessings are predicated? By its very geometry, there are no corners to be cut on the straight and narrow path.

How could one honor the moral agency of others without having the faith to develop significant patience and long-suffering? How could we behave redemptively without having developed the attributes of mercy and love?

To develop further all these cardinal and eternal qualities is to equip oneself for further service both now and in the world to come. In that world, as here, the focus of the Lord's work will be people; it will not shift suddenly to the manufacture of cosmic widgets!

If the cardinal virtues remain less developed in us we can, to be sure, still lead decent, useful, and honorable lives. But clearly we will be lacking in certain things. To the extent that here we have been diverted from those virtues, we have not been "valiant in the testimony of Jesus" (D&C 76:79).

His yoke, when fully and squarely placed upon us, is much lighter than the weight of sin. No burden is as heavy as the burden of the "natural man"! The annoying load of ambivalence and the hecticness of hesitation produce their own aggravations and frustrations.

Pride often blocks the path to the development of greater faith and the cardinal attributes essential to the man and woman of Christ. The best way to swallow our pride is to be "swallowed up" in the Father's will, as was Jesus: "The will of the son [was] swallowed up in the will of the Father"

(Mosiah 15:7). At the apogee of agony, though consumed with pain, Jesus was able to proceed because He was fully consumed in doing Father's will: "These things I have spoken unto you, that in me ye might have peace. In the world ye shall have tribulation: but be of good cheer; I have overcome the world." (John 16:33.)

He has set the pattern for us and shown us the way: "Saying, Father, if thou be willing, remove this cup from me: nevertheless not my will, but thine, be done" (Luke 22:42).

He had been thus committed for a long, long time: "And behold, I am the light and the life of the world; and I have drunk out of that bitter cup which the Father hath given me, and have glorified the Father in taking upon me the sins of the world, in the which I have suffered the will of the Father in all things from the beginning" (3 Nephi 11:11).

In Jesus' spiritual submissiveness there was the shining but subdued elegance of marvelous meekness. On our small scale initial meekness may consist of being willing simply to give place to develop that which is lacking in our faith.

We are not far into the process of giving place before we encounter our well-developed selfishness: Our schedule is too full to visit the sick. Other papers must be attended to before scriptures can be searched. Private prayers are put off till weariness limits both the quality and the quantity of our pleadings and appreciations. The cares of the world crowd out inward and reflective worship at a sacrament meeting.

Selfishness need not be gross in order to call the cadence in our lives. It merely needs to deflect us from thinking about an act of service to thinking about needing a new pair of shoes; or from making a nurturing phone call to watching a soap opera.

Sometimes our intentions lack full implementation because of waning energy. At other times an incipient righteous desire is overcome by pervasive fatigue. Good thoughts are dissolved by a loss of concentration amid weariness. Truly, "the spirit indeed is willing, but the flesh is weak" (Matthew 26:41). While we must beware of excusing ourselves too much, we do need to make some allowance for that fundamental fact.

Spiritual stimuli, for instance, can be choked out by the steady stimuli of the world. Thirst, hunger, fatigue — all can magnify the attractiveness of a mess of pottage.

As the Apostle Peter declared, we are in bondage to that which overcomes us (see 2 Peter 2:9). Such bondage is a needless burden and prevents happiness.

Selfishness, one type of bondage, magnifies our sufferings. In an early revelation of August 1831 the Lord warned Sidney Rigdon that he had "exalted himself in his heart, and received not counsel, but grieved the Spirit" (D&C 63:55). Sidney Rigdon's ego was not fully tamed. The Lord counseled him to "remain with my people" (D&C 124:104), but he did not.

Sidney Rigdon complained bitterly over his difficulties in Liberty Jail. These sufferings were real, but so was his stubborn self-pity. It elbowed out earlier and extraordinary spiritual experiences.

> Sidney was let out of the jail secretly at night, through the friendship of the sheriff and the jailor, "after having declared in prison that the sufferings of Jesus Christ were a fool to his," from which it appears that Sidney's sufferings, of the body and mind together, were almost more than he could bear (John Jaques, "Life and Labors of Sidney Rigdon," *Improvement Era*, February 1900, pp. 265–66).

Only six years after being lifted up by the Lord in the glorious theophany in Hiram, Ohio (see D&C 76), Sidney, though truly tried, felt put upon by the Lord! He first lost his heart and then his way.

To give place thus requires us to push wrong things out, including fear. Fear and faith are not good companions. The failure to give place, with all that that phrase implies, is usually part of what is lacking in the development of our faith.

As we put off more and more pride, thereby we can give place for more of the mulch of meekness in which faith grows steadily. Likewise, as we shed more selfishness, there is, for instance, more room to try the experiment of serving the sick. As Alma declared, each gospel principle, each gospel task, carries its own verifications and satisfactions.

But the tree of faith, though it grows quite quickly, nevertheless needs to be nourished "with great care" and over time, or it will wither. Though we gain direct knowledge in this or "in that thing, . . . neither must ye lay aside your faith" (Alma 32:34, 36).

The same things necessary to successfully planting the seed are necessary to the nourishment of the growing tree — worship, service, study, and prayer, with all of the specifics implicit in each of these.

When we search the scriptures we enlarge our memories (see Alma 37:8) by accessing the divine database instead of relying solely on our small set of experiences.

With regard to worship, prayer, study, and service, the words given to a king of Old Testament times should be observed: "Be strong, and do it" (1 Chronicles 28:10). The root system must be deep and wide to withstand wind and heat. If we "take no thought for its nourishment," this does not reflect on the quality of the seed or fruit. Rather, it reflects that "your ground is barren." What is ironical is that it is we who, when the tree withers, "pluck it up and cast it out." (Alma 32:38–39.) How many have so exited from the field of faith!

It takes faith to withstand the secular society. We who seek to serve in this day and time are, for instance, asked to be more loving at a time when the love of many waxes cold. We are asked to be more merciful, even as the Saints are persecuted. We are asked to be more holy as the world ripens in iniquity. We are asked to be more filled with hope in a world marked by growing despair because of growing iniquity. When, as in the world, there is more impatience, we are asked to be patient and full of faith even as other men's hearts fail them. We are asked to be peacemakers even as peace has been taken from the earth. We are asked to have enough faith to have fidelity in our marriage and chastity in dating even as the world celebrates sex almost as a secular religion.

As our people mature spiritually, however, we will reach the day foreseen by Nephi: "The power of the Lamb of God, . . . descended upon the saints of the church of the Lamb, and upon the covenant people of the Lord, who were scattered upon all the face of the earth; and they were armed with righteousness and with the power of God in great glory" (1 Nephi 14:14).

All this is to be accomplished in deteriorating circumstances such as are recorded in the ninth chapter of Moroni. For many people life is already without hope, without order, without mercy, without civilization. Many are already "past feeling" (Moroni 9:20). To perfect that which is lacking in our faith will be no small accomplishment!

Yet the Lord has promised that he will lead the man and woman of Christ across the gulf of misery and back to His heavenly kingdom.

Thus the Lord we worship is not an inscrutable and invisible force in the universe whose purposes are unclear. Instead, He is the loving Father who has told us specifically what His plan of happiness for us is and what our duties are.

Moreover, the more we keep the first great commandment, the more God will help us to keep the second great commandment. As for a time we experience His long-suffering, we are more inclined to extend our long-suffering to others. As we continue the journey of discipleship, more and more we will see things as they really are and also see people for who they really are. God's answers are abundant, and so are His instructive questions.

CHAPTER 9

"Answer This Question Yourselves"

The Lord has given us all the vital answers we need in order to be saved and to become men and women of Christ; in fact, "enough and to spare." But His questions are also revealing, as are the questions emanating from His prophets. As with those already noted in chapter 6, these questions also often contain implicit answers; they can brace us by reminding us of eternal realities.

Clearly the Lord uses questions for His teaching purposes: "Let us reason . . . with one another . . . that you may understand . . . wherefore, I the Lord ask you . . . this question" (D&C 50:11–13). Of many of His inquiries he might well say to us too, "Answer this question yourselves" (D&C 50:16). His questions are always deep in their implications; for instance, "Unto what were ye ordained?" He desires that we "answer" such questions so that we work through all the implications.

Think of it: Our Lord, who has created many worlds besides this one, having the patience and the love required to engage in such tutorials with seemingly insignificant individuals on this obscure planet at the edge of an ordinary sized galaxy!

Some of the special exchanges pile questions upon questions, all to the end that the Lord can more fully teach responsive persons. It is a mark not only of the Lord's love and patience but also of His long-suffering toward the learners. These tutorials show the Savior as the Master Teacher. He is always anxious to share more with us, as soon as we are ready.

Of course, as we consider inspired questions these are in contrast to our own foolish questions, which even God cannot answer. C. S. Lewis wrote: "All nonsense questions are unanswerable. How many hours are there in a mile? Is yellow square or round? Probably half the questions we ask —half of our great theological and metaphysical problems —are like that." (*A Mind Awake* [New York: Harcourt, Brace, and World, 1968], p. 61.)

We can also avoid answering inspired searching questions. We can likewise hedge in our responses to searching questions. But if we possess meekness, this meekness will supply the readiness to hear and to learn.

Being humble enough to ask inspired and significant questions is important. Elias Higbee's sincere question about what is meant by Isaiah 52:1 (see D&C 113:7) would not be on a par with the questions of Enoch and Joseph Smith inquiring why God can weep (see Moses 7:29) and asking Him "Where is the pavilion that covereth thy hiding place?" (D&C 121:1.) There is no democracy among our questions.

Some questions are asked not for information but to put our verification on the record: "And he said unto them, When I sent you without purse, and scrip, and shoes, lacked ye any thing? And they said, Nothing." (Luke 22:35.) Confirmations put reminders on the record, and they sober and instruct us for what lies ahead (see Luke 22:36–38).

Why not, therefore, take full advantage of the answers contained in the tutoring questions and their emerging and instructive one-liners from the Lord? Though asked of others, these questions are full of generic insights and needed directions for us as well as for the actual addressees.

The questions asked by the Lord also tell us much about the questioner and His substance and style, which we are to emulate. Thus these interrogatories are placed in the holy scriptures to inspire us, to encourage us, and to be pondered by us.

While some of the episodes cited involve corrective counsel, given long ago to individuals, surely in the elapsing years the meek among those individuals have long since worked things through with the Lord. Thus we are not "picking" on people when we cite them as examples; rather, we are trying to identify correct principles in order to help us with our own deficiencies. Therefore, since these episodes have been preserved for us for a wise purpose, let us so use them—but without being unduly judgmental of, or condescending toward, the individuals involved.

One superlative illustration of how the Lord used questions to instruct the improving disciple is His exchange with Enoch. The Lord and Enoch "reason with one another," that Enoch "may understand." Enoch bore record that he actually saw the God of heaven weep. Indeed, the heavens "shed forth their tears as the rain upon the mountains." Perplexed Enoch then asked how God, involved with "millions of earths like this," could weep. (Moses 7:28–31.)

In response, the Lord rehearsed events from the time of the Garden of Eden, telling that, despite being commanded to love one another, many people had become "without affection," and that instead of choosing Him, many had chosen Satan as their father—hence, "misery shall be their doom." The Lord then answered Enoch's question with a question: "Wherefore should not the heavens weep, seeing these shall suffer?" (Moses 7:32–37.) The Lord, long-suffering and loving, weeps over needless human suffering and misery.

Enoch wept, too. At first he "refuse[d] to be comforted." But in His mercy the Lord gave Enoch further perspective: "Lift up your heart, and be glad; and look." Enoch then saw the forthcoming day of the great rescuing mission of Jesus, His atoning sacrifice, and the Resurrection. And the Lord described to him the restoration of the gospel in the last days and the other events associated with His second coming, and showed Enoch "all things even unto the end of the world." (Moses 7:41–67.)

In difficult moments as we witness needless human suffering, such perspective can and should comfort us, too. Nor need we be immobilized by human suffering. Ever since God gave "unto man his agency" (Moses 7:32), avoidable human misery has been largely caused by wrong choices and wrong behavior. Without gospel perspective, however, some cite human misery as a reason to doubt or to deny God. Failing to understand God's plan, some even imply their own moral superiority because, unlike God, they really "care" about human suffering!

In His exchange with Enoch, the mercy and love of God and certain causes of mortal misery are made abundantly clear. Even so, God will not suspend His "plan of happiness," though man's misuse of moral agency causes such gross human misery. There is no other way.

At yet another level of significance, our unmeek questions reveal the need for our further tutoring. In this dispensation the Lord warned that one might "do many mighty works, yet if he boasts in his own strength . . . he must fall" (D&C 3:4). This declaration parallels an ancient lesson: "And [Moses] said unto them, Hear now, ye rebels; must *we* fetch you water out of this rock?" (Numbers 20:10, italics added.)

President Spencer W. Kimball observed: "Moses had integrity in great measure, but in that unguarded moment he had presumptuously taken credit for the Lord's miracle." (*Faith Precedes the Miracle* [Salt Lake City: Deseret Book Company, 1972], p. 243.)

The pronoun-problem "we" reflected a momentary confusion about causality. It also reflected Moses' understandable fatigue, weariness, and exasperation. Instead of considering each case anew with fresh empathy and resolve, busy, weary priesthood leaders conducting "back-to-back" interviews can likewise be similarly rushed, pressed, fatigued. The flesh is weak, and as a result we say and do things we would not if we were fresh and meek, or if we had time to ponder and to remember.

Our Lord, though full of empathy, nevertheless asked weary Apostles, "Couldest not thou watch one hour?" (Mark 14:37.) Some moments transcend not only our energy but also our capacity to appreciate. Some supernal opportunities seem too big to be taken easy advantage of, especially as mortal frailties assert themselves.

The most sobering questions are often also the most brief, as when the Lord asked, "What is property unto me?" (D&C 117:4.) Can we become men and women of Christ if property means too much to us? The Lord continued with yet another question involving perspective: "[Why] covet that which is but the drop, and neglect the more weighty matters?" (D&C 117:8.) Oh, how we need this precious perspective!

Perceptive questions have a special way of framing the moments that matter, eliciting answers and responses otherwise unproferred. Meekly responded to, honest questions may also provide opportunities for full spiritual surrender to the Lord.

In the honest questions Enoch, Moses, and others asked of the Lord there was a sense of unpreparedness but not an unwillingness. Prophets do feel their inadequacies: Enoch asked of the Lord: "Why is it that I have found favor in thy sight, and am but a lad, and all the people hate me; for I am slow of speech; wherefore am I thy servant?" (Moses 6:3.)

Moses said to God, "Who am I, that I should go unto Pharaoh, and that I should bring forth the children of Israel out of Egypt?" (Exodus 3:11.) Subsequently, after experiencing difficulty, "Moses returned unto the Lord, and said, Lord, . . . why is it that thou hast sent me?" (Exodus 5:22.) Nevertheless, after some needed tutoring, Moses loyally did as he was divinely bidden, just as did Enoch!

Yet another episode shows the role of an inspired question in evoking surrender: "And Aaron answered him and said unto him: Believest thou that there is a God? And the king said: I know that the Amalekites say that there is a God, and I have granted unto them that they should build sanctuaries, that they may assemble themselves together to worship him. And if now thou sayest there is a God, behold I will believe." (Alma 22:7.)

The questioning facilitated the king's disclosing what really bothered him: "Behold, this is the thing which doth trouble me" (Alma 22:5). How often in our ministering to the people do we get at what is really troubling them? If we questioned more often under the direction of the Spirit, then we too could help others more often to surrender.

Much as with Saul of Tarsus, questions were asked of another whom the Lord needed to rescue by crisp inquiry. "Alma, rise and stand forth, for why persecutest thou the church of God?" (Mosiah 27:13.) Again we witness the directness and the first-name personal-ness of the Lord's entreaties.

When in Egypt, Joseph successfully resisted temptation, showing how instructive the questions of the meek can be. After rehearsing his loyalties to God and to Potiphar, Joseph asked Potiphar's wife a searching question; it was drenched with integrity: "How then can I do this great wickedness, and sin against God?" (Genesis 39:9.)

Even early on when Jesus was a lad, He was found in the temple asking learned doctors questions (see Luke 2:46). Not only did Jesus, the lad, ask questions of the learned in the temple, but upon receiving reproof from His anxious mother He also asked her and Joseph a profound question: "And he said unto them, How is it that ye sought me? wist ye not that I must be about my Father's business?" (Luke 2:49.) He knew so much, so young, including how to put tutoring questions.

Later on, His deft and inspired questions exposed hypocrisy:

> And Jesus answered and said unto them, I will also ask of you one question, and answer me, and I will tell you by what authority I do these things.
>
> The baptism of John, was it from heaven, or of men? answer me.
>
> And they reasoned with themselves, saying, If we shall say, From heaven; he will say, Why then did ye not believe him?
>
> But if we shall say, Of men; they feared the people: for all men counted John, that he was a prophet indeed.
>
> And they answered and said unto Jesus, We cannot tell. And Jesus answering saith unto them, Neither do I tell you by what authority I do these things. (Mark 11:29-33.)

The questions Nephi asked of Laman and Lemuel reveal not only his perspective about the Lord's competency but also his capacity to remember. It was just the opposite with Laman and Lemuel, who did not want to risk venturing into Laban's "establishment" in order to get the brass plates. Noting that Laban was a "mighty man" and could slay them, skeptically they asked Nephi, "How is it possible that the Lord will deliver Laban into our hands?" (1 Nephi 3:31.) In response Nephi asked, "[Since] the Lord is mightier than all the earth, then why not mightier than Laban and his fifty, yea, or even than his tens of thousands?" (1 Nephi 4:1.)

The difference in individual perspective among these three was further illustrated: "And it came to pass that I, Nephi, said unto my father: I will go and do the things which the Lord hath commanded, for I know that the Lord giveth no commandments unto the children of men, save he shall prepare a way for them that they may accomplish the thing which he commandeth them" (1 Nephi 3:7).

Still further illumination as to his intellectual integrity is shown by Nephi's likewise asking the brothers: "Wherefore can ye doubt? Let us go up; the Lord is able to deliver us, even as our fathers, and to destroy Laban, even as the Egyptians." (1 Nephi 4:3.)

Forgotten spiritual experiences are no help, either. Nephi asked Laman and Lemuel, "How is it that ye have forgotten that ye have seen an angel of the Lord?" who had delivered them out of Laban's hands (1 Nephi 7:10; see also 1 Nephi 7:11).

Laman and Lemuel's different spiritual disposition is evident from many comments in the record, such as, "They did not look unto the Lord as they ought" (1 Nephi 15:3).

Amid their disputations, Nephi asked Laman and Lemuel a simple question that revealed his trust in a simple process: "Have ye inquired of the Lord?" (1 Nephi 15:8.) Laman and Lemuel represent a vast army of humans to whom the idea of inquiring of the Lord does not even occur as an option!

The questions we ask can make plain our paucity of perspective. One of the reasons why Esau was willing to sell his birthright is disclosed thus: "Behold, I am at the point to die: and what profit shall this birthright do to me?" (Genesis 25:32.) If Esau saw his birthright as pertaining only to this life, he surely did not have an eternal perspective! Faith, after all, involves perspectives that stretch both ways —beyond today by remembering of the past, and by extrapolating our faith into the future. Such is part of both the utility and the beauty of faith: a mess of pottage remains a mess of pottage and no more.

The fact that the wicked often seem to profit and do very well in this life may fill us with questions: "Ye have said, It is vain to serve God: and what profit is it that we have kept his ordinance, and that we have walked mournfully before the Lord of hosts?" (Malachi 3:14.)

Yet is it not true that "the triumphing of the wicked is short, and the joy of the hypocrite but for a moment?" (Job

20:5.) The Lord Himself confirmed that those who follow the ways of man have "joy in their works [but] for a season" (3 Nephi 27:11).

Inspired questions often bring forth immediate and inspired one-liners, as in these responses to questions.

> And Samuel said, Hath the Lord as great delight in burnt offerings and sacrifices, as in obeying the voice of the Lord? Behold, to obey is better than sacrifice, and to hearken than the fat of rams. (1 Samuel 15:22.)

> And he said unto me: Knowest thou the condescension of God?
> And I said unto him: I know that [God] loveth his children; nevertheless, I do not know the meaning of all things. (1 Nephi 11:16–17.)

An inspired question may also be followed by a telling silence! "How long halt ye between two opinions? If the Lord be God, follow him, but if Baal, follow him. And the people answered him not a word." (1 Kings 18:21.)

Insightful questions can call forth major doctrinal insights: "And his disciples asked him, saying, Master, who did sin, this man, or his parents, that he was born blind?" And the answer: "Neither . . . but that the works of God should be made manifest in him." (John 9:2, 3.)

Questions by those in distress may draw forth divine reassurance about God's plans and His timing, because real faith in God includes faith in His timing. Job asked, "Is there not an appointed time to man upon earth?" (Job 7:1.) Near the end of his life, Joseph Smith was reassured that his life would not be cut unprovidently short: "Thy days are known, and thy years will not be numbered less" (D&C 122:9).

Our human worth is raised in various questions: "What is man, that thou shouldest magnify him? and that thou shouldest set thine heart upon him?" (Job 7:17.) Throughout holy scripture we see how valued we actually are. God does desire to magnify us! His heart is set upon us! We are the sheep of His fold and the people of His pasture! (See Psalm 95:7.) We are His spirit sons and daughters! (D&C 93:23, 29; Hebrews 12:9; Moses 3:5; 6:36, 51.)

Divine determination is noted in this question: "He is in one mind, and who can turn him? And what his soul desireth, even that he doeth." (Job 23:13.) A matching reflection is found in the Book of Abraham: "There is nothing that the Lord thy God shall take in his heart to do but what he will do it" (Abraham 3:17).

Meek individuals, being humble, are introspective enough to ask searching questions which set the stage for insights that should lift us all. "O then, if I have seen so great things, if the Lord in his condescension unto the children of men hath visited men in so much mercy, why should my heart weep and my soul linger in the valley of sorrow, and my flesh waste away, and my strength slacken, because of mine afflictions?" (2 Nephi 4:26.)

Nephi continued his productive introspection: "And why should I yield to sin, because of my flesh? Yea, why should I give way to temptations, that the evil one have place in my heart to destroy my peace and afflict my soul? Why am I angry because of mine enemy?" Then came his pleading questions to the Lord: "O Lord, wilt thou redeem my soul? Wilt thou deliver me out of the hands of mine enemies? Wilt thou make me that I may shake at the appearance of sin?" (2 Nephi 4:27, 31.) The interplay of feelings and pleadings clearly occurs in the framework of faith.

Joseph Smith was similarly introspective, apparently even in his youth: "In the midst of this war of words and tumult of opinions, I often said to myself: What is to be done? Who of all these parties are right; or, are they all wrong together? If any one of them be right, which is it, and how shall I know it?" (Joseph Smith—History 1:10.)

After the great vision, badgered and persecuted, Joseph pondered: "Why should the powers of darkness combine against me?" "Why the opposition and persecution that arose against me, almost in my infancy?" And again: "Why persecute me for telling the truth? I have actually seen a vision; and who am I that I can withstand God, or why does the world think to make me deny what I have actually seen?" (Joseph Smith—History 1:20, 25.) The Prophet Joseph Smith was a man of great depth of feeling; he knew much poignancy!

Questions are sometimes asked in order to prepare the way for immediate responses. Nephi asked how it was that Jesus "did fulfill all righteousness in being baptized by water?" (2 Nephi 31:6.) Nephi then instructed and declared that this was accomplished by Jesus' "[showing] unto the children of men that, according to the flesh he humbleth himself before the Father, and witnesseth unto the Father that he would be obedient unto him in keeping his commandments." Nephi quickly and trenchantly asked: "Can we follow Jesus save we shall be willing to keep the commandments of the Father?" (2 Nephi 31:7, 10.) Jesus fully humbled himself before the Father by experiencing many things "according to the flesh," and we must do likewise.

Our focus should, therefore, always be on our great example, Jesus: "For how knoweth a man the master whom he has not served, and who is a stranger unto him, and is far from the thoughts and intents of his heart?" (Mosiah 5:13.) What brings us closer to Jesus than pondering His marvelous atonement? Articulate Jacob asked, "Why not speak of the atonement of Christ, and attain to a perfect knowledge of him, as to attain to the knowledge of a resurrection and the world to come?" (Jacob 4:12.) Why, Jacob inquired in lamentation, do people reject the words of the prophets about Christ, "deny the good word of Christ, and the power of God, and the gift of the Holy Ghost, and quench the Holy Spirit, and make a mock of the great plan of redemption?" (Jacob 6:8.) Why, indeed?

Prophets often ask diagnostic questions in order to determine the status of people's spiritual knowledge. Paul, for instance, determined through questions that some followers of John the Baptist needed to be instructed (see Acts 19:1–6; see also 18:25).

Other deep, diagnostic questions asked by prophets are represented by this instance: "And now behold, I ask you, my brethren of the church, have ye spiritually been born of God? Have ye received his image in your countenances? Have ye experienced this mighty change in your hearts?" (Alma 5:14.)

Questions evoke responses that provide instruction but also prepare the way for further instruction, as when Ammon asked the king, "Believest thou that there is a God?" After their colloquy, the king both declared and then further inquired, "I believe all these things which thou hast spoken. Art thou sent from God?" (Alma 18:24, 33.)

In questioning, even nostalgia can be very useful, hence, "I would ask, can ye feel so now?" (Alma 5:26.) Lapsed faith may be revived by probing the past, especially by reconnoitering the reservoir of happy memories.

It should not surprise us if some questions are repeated from dispensation to dispensation: "Behold, are ye stripped of pride?" "Behold, I say, is there one among you who is not stripped of envy?" (Alma 5:28, 29.) And in 1831 the Lord said, "Strip yourselves from jealousies . . . and humble yourselves before me, for ye are not sufficiently humble" (D&C 67:10).

The Lord asked this next question not only of Abraham but also of Jeremiah: "Behold I am the Lord, the God of all flesh: is there any thing too hard for me?" (Jeremiah 32:27; see also Genesis 18:14.) A question which is also an answer!

It is not surprising that the pleadings of the prophets are often similar. Alma "lifted up his voice to heaven and cried, saying: O, how long, O Lord, wilt thou suffer that thy servants shall dwell here below in the flesh, to behold such gross wickedness among the children of men? . . . O Lord God, how long wilt thou suffer that such wickedness and infidelity shall be among this people? O Lord, wilt thou give me strength, that I may bear with mine infirmities?" (Alma 31:26, 30.) These poignant pleadings are strikingly parallel to those pleadings of Joseph Smith emanating from Liberty Jail:

> O God, where art thou? And where is the pavilion that covereth thy hiding place?
>
> How long shall thy hand be stayed, and thine eye, yea thy pure eye, behold from the eternal heavens the wrongs of thy people and of thy servants, and thine ear be penetrated with their cries?
>
> Yea, O Lord, how long shall they suffer these wrongs and unlawful oppressions, before thine heart shall be softened toward them, and thy bowels be moved with compassion toward them? (D&C 121:1-3.)

Such introspective questions can reflect a readiness to learn, an inner meekness: "And they said one to another, Did not our heart burn within us, while he talked with us by the way, and while he opened to us the scriptures?" (Luke 24:32.) Being honest with ourselves is vital.

The repetitiveness and the routineness of life are emphasized a number of times in the scriptures. The expressions concerning eating, drinking, and giving in marriage convey this sameness and routineness.

Jesus declared "as it was in the days of Noah, so it shall be also at the coming of the Son of Man" (Joseph Smith—Matthew 1:41). People will be eating and drinking and giving in marriage, being overcome and consumed by the routineness and repetitiveness of daily life devoid of spiritual context. This is a terrible waste of one's mortal probation. There can be much more to life—much, much more!

Indeed, the pursuit of such routineness is not enough! Jesus pointedly asked, "Is not the life more than meat, and the body than raiment?" (3 Nephi 13:25.)

Before He asks, the Lord knows when we are puzzled and also unlikely to give good responses, so He teaches us if we have ears to hear: "Therefore, why is it that ye cannot understand and know that he that receiveth the word by the Spirit of truth receiveth it as it is preached by the Spirit of truth?" (D&C 50:21.)

The same tutorial pattern appears in His asking, "Unto what shall I liken these kingdoms, that ye may understand?" (D&C 88:46.) We are then treated to an expansive, panoramic view of things. This should leave us breathless as to the universality of the Lord's work, for "any man who hath seen any or the least of these hath seen God moving in his majesty and power" (D&C 88:47).

Short questions are often introductions to longer and profound answers. A special example is this: "Behold, there are many called, but few are chosen. And why are they not chosen?" (D&C 121:34.) Lest this seem a "hard saying" (John 6:60), we are then treated to specific and sobering insights from the Lord about why only few are chosen (see D&C 121:34–46). This elaboration is given nowhere else in scripture! It is a significant part of the fulness of the Restoration and includes counsel on how human foibles can keep us from gaining access to the powers of heaven and how power and authority are to be exercised. In the New Testament, on the other hand, only Jesus' terse, seemingly deterministic statement is preserved, "Many are called, but few are chosen" (Matthew 22:14; see also 20:16).

Questions asked of the Lord involving vital, doctrinal instruction occur as early as Adam: "Why is it that men must repent and be baptized in water?" The response to that question was followed by needed instruction and by marvelous assurance: "And the Lord said unto Adam: Behold I have forgiven thee thy transgression in the Garden of Eden" (Moses 6:53).

The Lord once asked: "Am I a God at hand, . . . and not a God afar off?" (Jeremiah 23:23.)

Surely He is both, as observed by Enoch, who saw God's vast creations and His weeping, yet exclaimed, "Yet thou art there" (Moses 7:30). God, whose "curtains are stretched out," can bring to pass, as He has done, the removal of a mere mortal "iron curtain." Indeed, "All things must come to pass in their time" (see D&C 64:32). He needs our meekness, however, in order to part the curtains of our understanding.

If we understand the profound implications of our beliefs, real brotherhood is possible: "Have we not all one father? Hath not one God created us? Why do we deal treacherously every man against his brother?" (Malachi 2:10.) On this relationship, apostolic assurance is given us: "And [God] hath made of one blood all nations of men for to dwell on all the face of the earth, and hath determined the times before appointed, and the bounds of their habitation" (Acts 17:26).

And on the "dealing treacherously," Nephi wrote:

> For none of these iniquities come of the Lord; for he doeth that which is good among the children of men; and he doeth nothing save it be plain unto the children of men; and he inviteth them all to come unto him and partake of his goodness; and he denieth none that come unto him, black and white, bond and free, male and female; and he remembereth the heathen; and all are alike unto God, both Jew and Gentile (2 Nephi 26:33).

As we hear the Lord's answers, they are not always easy to bear. For example, Jesus' discourse on the dangers of wealth produced anxiety and inquiry among His followers: "When his disciples heard it, they were exceedingly amazed, saying, Who then can be saved?" (Matthew 19:25.) Note the Savior's response as rendered by the Joseph Smith Translation: "But Jesus beheld their thoughts, and said unto them, With men this is impossible; but if they will forsake all things for my sake, with God whatsoever things I speak are possible" (JST, Matthew 19:26). We can succeed, if we will forsake the world. Otherwise the soul-stretching, mind-expanding demands of the gospel would be impossible to meet. To have one's soul "greatly enlarge[d] without hypocrisy" (D&C 121:42) is part of the journey of discipleship.

Perhaps no question was more terse while eliciting more magnificent though brief responses than when God the Father said of His plan of salvation and of the need for a Savior, "Whom shall I send?" "Here am I, send me." (Abraham 3:27.) The rest is supernal history!

The more we understand the virtues and attributes of God, the more we see that the ways of the natural man and woman have no place in heaven: "Know ye not that the unrighteous shall not inherit the kingdom of God? Be not deceived: neither fornicators, nor idolaters, nor adulterers, nor effeminate, nor abusers of themselves with mankind . . . shall inherit the kingdom of God." (1 Corinthians 6:9–10.)

The natural man, however, does not like counsel from a man of Christ. Paul asked, "Am I therefore become your enemy, because I tell you the truth?" (Galatians 4:16.) In contrast, the children of Christ, who are in the process of growing up to a fulness of the stature of Christ, will surely be tutored: "If ye endure chastening, God dealeth with you as with sons; for what son is he whom the father chasteneth not?" (Hebrews 12:7.)

There are great, unanswered questions — at least, unanswered at the time: "And about the ninth hour Jesus cried with a loud voice, saying, Eli, Eli, lama sabachthani? that is to say, My God, my God, why hast thou forsaken me?" (Matthew 27:46.) On our small scale we too may go without immediate answers in our pleadings of distress.

If we regard our Father and Redeemer rightly and with gratitude, we will savor their questions and accept all their answers.

CHAPTER 10

"Glory Be to the Father"

More often than we do as men and women aspiring to become more like His firstborn, we might profitably pause to ponder *all* the Father has done for us. Among so many things are the following reminders that should spur our quest to become men and women of Christ:

1. As part of His plan of happiness, He did whatever was required to move us from our earliest state of being on into spirit entities with individual spirit bodies; thus we truly became His spirit sons and daughters.

2. He thus became the Father of our spirits, an ever-loving, everlasting, exemplary Father.

3. He organized this world just for us.

4. He has subsequently given our spirits mortal bodies; and one day, after the resurrection, bodies and spirits will be permanently united and the righteous will have a fulness of joy. This fulness of joy is part of the plan of happiness He has provided for us.

5. He has given us families, prophets, scriptures, and temples, all to help prepare us to return to Him, thus sharing with us the very secrets of the universe.
6. Eventually He will give to the faithful "all that He hath."

Thus we see that Father's love is expressed in many profound and significant ways. No wonder He is described as "merciful and gracious" (D&C 76:5). No wonder the Apostle John told us God so loved the world that He gave us His Son to lead us to eternal life (John 3:16). The Book of Mormon declares that God loves the world and does nothing save it be "for the benefit of the world" (2 Nephi 26:24). Even when we come to truly love Him, the fact is that He loved us first! (1 John 4:19.)

How often, in our private prayers, do we thank Heavenly Father for any of the above-enumerated things? Or are we so busy petitioning Him for the new and pressing needs of the moment that we forget past blessings and His promised blessings of eternity? In recording the revelation he received on October 3, 1918, President Joseph F. Smith spoke of the "wonderful love made manifest by the Father and the Son" (D&C 138:3). "Oh, it is wonderful!"

We can all join an ancient prophet in his tender expression of gratitude to God as he approached death. This servant of God observed, "I am encircled about eternally in the arms of his love" (2 Nephi 1:15).

No wonder young Jesus noted that He must be about His Father's profound and rescuing business. Only modern revelation describes specifically and grandly what that unique loving and rescuing business is: "This is my work and my glory — to bring to pass the immortality and eternal life of man" (Moses 1:39).

Jesus has always gladly given all glory to our generous Father. God the Father and Jesus are far more generous toward the faithful than anything the latter could rightly ask of them, including their lifting the faithful up "at the last day" (3 Nephi 27:22). And "the tender mercies of the Lord are over all those whom he hath chosen, because of their faith" (1 Nephi 1:20).

In contrast, the adversary will not support his dutiful followers at the last day (see Alma 30:60).

Our Father delights to honor those who serve Him! (See D&C 76:5.) He even weeps over needless human suffering: "And it came to pass that the God of heaven looked upon the residue of the people, and he wept; and Enoch bore record of it, saying: How is it that the heavens weep, and shed forth their tears as the rain upon the mountains?" (Moses 7:28.)

God not only keeps His promises but in doing so rewards very generously. His windows of heaven are opened wide to pour out blessings in response to our tithe of a mere one-tenth! (See Malachi 3:10.)

Both premortally and after the astonishing atonement, Jesus said "Glory be to the Father" (see Moses 4:2; D&C 19:19). What a contrast to those of us unprofitable servants who, after doing a few good deeds, insist on keeping score!

We worry over whether or not our little deed is noticed. We notice the size of the letters on the mortal marquees over the tiny little theaters where our "own little plot is always being played."

We continue to be overly concerned with getting mortal credit and over-establishing our worth. As God's children we do have great value and genuine intrinsic, individual worth. Must that intrinsic worth ever be at the mercy of our moods or of extrinsic, ephemeral measuring rods?

In contrast, Jesus declared:

Behold, I am Jesus Christ, whom the prophets testified shall come into the world.

And behold, I am the light and the life of the world; and I have drunk out of that bitter cup which the Father hath given me, and have glorified the Father in taking upon me the sins of the world, in the which I have suffered the will of the Father in all things from the beginning. (3 Nephi 11:10-11.)

How could we have any greater recognition anyway than that of being a spirit son or daughter of God? or of finally deserving to be known as a man or woman of Christ? How could we possibly ever be given more than "all that my Father hath"? There isn't any more!

No matter how much we do, we will never be able even to approach, let alone match, the goodness of God and all that He has done and will do for us. Therefore, of that portion which has been allotted to us in this life, why should we desire more? Especially in view of what lies ahead for the faithful. (See Alma 29:6.)

The revelations about our true identity tell us of our immense possibilities. These revelations may irritate some contemporaries, as happened earlier when Jesus disclosed His identity: "Therefore the Jews sought the more to kill him, because he not only had broken the sabbath, but said also that God was his Father, making himself equal with God" (John 5:18). Wrong as they were about some things, they nevertheless understood that a "son" is of the same essence as his father. So it is with our being God's spirit children.

If fully faithful, we will receive of His fulness, for He has told us: "I give unto you these sayings that you may understand and know how to worship, and know what you worship, that you may come unto the Father in my name, and in due time receive of his fulness" (D&C 93:19). This is one of the great but under-appreciated blessings of the restored gospel. It richly assures us of our intrinsic value and of our eternal and ultimate worth. Therefore we need not be entirely dependent upon human assessments and evaluations. In any case, if recognition arising from proximate circumstances based upon fleeting criteria constitutes the sole measure of our personal significance, recognition will be both mercurial and insufficient. The Lord's recognition, however, is enduring. Note that while a new king came along who knew not Joseph (Exodus 1:8), God knew and valued Joseph, as an individual, long before and long after any Pharaohs ever existed.

Peers may not always pay heed to us, but the meek can abide this neglect and even their disdain. Colleagues may not always value what we say. But God actually listens to our prayers. He is perfect in both justice and mercy (see Mosiah 16:1; 27:31; Alma 12:15). He knows perfectly the very thoughts and the real intents of our hearts—he never misunderstands us.

The temporal causes which we champion may fail—after all we can do. But God's work of which we are part will finally triumph! He is remarkably able to do His own work, just as He has so directly stated (see 2 Nephi 27:20-21). Indeed, we are at the very center of His work. In the hassling competition of the work of the world we may lose out. But we always win when we lose ourselves in God's service.

In the worthy work of the world, mortals will have "joy in [their] works for a season" (3 Nephi 27:11). But everlasting and full joy comes only with God's gift of eternal life. Granted, when we are in the service of our fellowmen we are in the service of God (Mosiah 2:17). But the more we do of spiritual significance, the greater the significance of service.

Events may turn against us, but if we are turning ever more toward God, we are on course. This is the only turning that really matters. Though that turning may bring with it an attendant churning, better the spiritual churning of a broken heart than an unyielding, hard heart.

Friends may betray us, but Jesus never fails us. He even calls us his friends; the Father and Jesus are our best and only perfect friends (see John 15:14, 15; D&C 84:77; 93:45).

Illustrative of how God is a true Father who desires maximum, eternal happiness for His children, we are advised that on occasion God will chasten his people and will try our patience and faith (see Mosiah 23:21). Is not the question, "Why, O Lord?" one which goes to the heart of the further development of faith amid tutoring? Similarly, is not the question, "How long, O Lord?" one which goes to the very heart of developing patience amid tutoring? Thus we see how interactive all of these things are in the developmental dimensions of God's plan of salvation, which culminates in eternal life.

When we err, others may be unforgiving and ungenerous. But though our sins be as scarlet, God assures the repentant that these shall be as white as snow (see Isaiah 1:18). Moreover, God will not even mention certain portions of our past (Ezekiel 18:22). In that case, nor should we! It should be hand to the plow without looking back. Finally, He mercifully assures us that if we repent He actually will remember our sins no more! (D&C 58:42.)

God's remarkable redemptiveness and His stunning personal-ness occur amid His governance of the expanding galaxies. "Yet," as Enoch comfortingly exclaimed of God, "thou art there."

The Father has promised the faithful "all that [He] hath" (D&C 84:38). How bounteously we will then be "added upon"! (See Abraham 3:26.) Compare His "all" to a vied-for promotion in a company which will not even exist ten years from now. Or to an envied place in the hierarchy of an organizational chart which will be scrambled again in six months.

Occasionally we see those who do something bad justify it on the grounds that thereby they can thereafter do some good: "If I can just make this deal or gain this office, think of the position I will be in to do much good." This rationalizing might be called looking beyond Lucifer's shoulder—on to imagined possibilities. It is a very different thing from saying, "Get thee behind me!" (See Matthew 16:23.)

Sometimes we scarcely know what to petition God for (see Romans 8:26). At other times we do not realize the implications of what we ask for (see Matthew 20:22). The eye of faith sees things as they really are (see Jacob 4:13; see also Alma 5:15); yet at other times our eyes may actually be "holden," because we are not ready for divine disclosure (see Luke 24:16). At still other times the scales fall, giving us eyes to see (see 2 Nephi 30:6).

There are many sincere searchers after truth and wisdom, as represented in this expression by Will Durant: "So much of our lives is meaningless, . . . but we would believe all the while that there is something vital and significant in us. . . . We want to seize the value and perspective of passing things, and so to pull ourselves up out of the maelstrom of daily circumstance. We want to know that the little things are little, and the big things big, before it is too late; we want to see things now as they will seem forever—'in the light of eternity.' " (*The Story of Philosophy* [Garden City, N.Y.: Garden City Publishing Co., 1943], p. 1.) Christian disciples understand that the illumination will come through revelation.

And what "seeing" there will be one day! "That which is of God is light; and he that receiveth light, and continueth in God, receiveth more light; and that light groweth brighter and brighter until the perfect day" (D&C 50:24).

Before God's throne we will bow in humble reverence! Whatever our spiritual progress may be in the future—even though we receive "all that the Father hath"—throughout eternity we will never cease praising Him in humble reverence and giving Him "glory forever and ever" for all that He has done for us. (See D&C 76:93.)

At the judgment we will not only have the Book of Mormon's prophesied "bright recollection" and "perfect remembrance" of our misdeeds (see Alma 5:18; 11:43). The joyous things will be preserved too—we shall know "even as we know now" (Alma 11:43; see also D&C 93:33). Among the "all things [that] shall be restored" (Alma 40:23) will be memory, including eventually the memory of premortal events and conditions. What a flood of feeling and fact will come to us when, at a time a loving God deems wise, this faculty is restored! Surely it will increase our gratefulness for God's long-suffering and for Jesus' atonement! Hence one of the great blessings of immortality and eternal life will be the joy of our being connected again with the memories of both the first and the second estates.

Oh, how great is our God! "Yea, and how is it that ye have forgotten that the Lord is able to do all things according to his will, for the children of men, if it so be that they exercise faith in him? Wherefore, let us be faithful to him." (1 Nephi 7:12.)

He is surely able to do his own work (see 2 Nephi 27:20–21). His purposes will all—indeed must—come to pass in their time (see D&C 64:32). And as his children we should be happy to be at the center of His loving purposes.

May we return to Him in full reconciliation as true sons and daughters, as men and women of Christ.

Glory be to the Father!

Subject Index

Scripture Index

OLD TESTAMENT

NEW TESTAMENT

BOOK OF MORMON

DOCTRINE AND COVENANTS

PEARL OF GREAT PRICE